MINISTER
ON
THE
SPOT

MINISTER
ON
THE
SPOT

James E. Dittes

PILGRIM PRESS PHILADELPHIA BOSTON

SBN 8298-0155-3

Copyright © 1970 United Church Press

Library of Congress Catalog Card Number 79-114051

CONTENTS

38
YEARS
ON
THE
VERGE

Now there is in Jerusalem by the Sheep Gate a pool,
in Hebrew called Beth-za'tha, which has five porticoes.
In these lay a multitude of invalids, blind, lame, paralyzed.
One man was there, who had been ill for thirty-eight
years. When Jesus saw him and knew that he had been
lying there a long time, he said to him, "Do you want to
be healed?" The sick man answered him, "Sir, I have no
man to put me into the pool when the water is troubled,
and while I am going another steps down before me." Jesus said to him, "Rise, take up your pallet, and walk." And
at once the man was healed, and he took up his pallet
and walked.

John 5:2–9

Only a few steps away, in the surging waters of the pool,
there is healing, vitality, strength, a new life. But the man lies
ill *beside* the pool, separated from health and restoration by
only a few steps, but separated also, decisively and tragically,
by his own resignation to what he thinks is his destiny: "Vitality is there, and I am here, and we are separated, perhaps
trivially, but unbridgeably. I don't have the help I need to
change things, and anyway somebody else always beats me

1

to it. My lot is to be here, on the verge, not there in the midst of vitality. Other people are in the swim, but I must watch from the edges."

Jesus' answer seems to be something like this: While you are waiting and watching and ruing the distance between yourself and immersion into the creative and healing forces, while you may feel on the verge, you are really already fully in the midst of these forces. "Rise, take up your pallet, and walk." When you feel most immobilized before urgent needs and expectations—a minister on the spot—exactly then and there you may be in the best position to make your move, to minister on the spot.

Thirty-eight years must be close to the average length of a man's ministry. How many of those years are spent on the verge? How many of those years are spent waiting and watching, waiting for the extra help, the extra training, the extra experience, the right moment, the right circumstances which will immerse one fully in God's healing work among men? How much of a day, how much of a career is spent watching from a distance, perhaps great, perhaps tormentingly small, while others seem to be fully immersed in significant ministry? How many of those years are spent waiting with the rueful sense of separation between oneself and the significant currents of events in God's world and man's?

In the Halloween preparations in our home recently, the oldest attempted to initiate the youngest with talk of terror, of witches and goblins that roamed abroad in the dark. But the youngest was undaunted, "If *I'm* there, they won't be real." This remark may be 10 percent bravado, but it's at least 90 percent self-deprecation. "If I'm there, they won't be real." There may well be such magnificent and splendid and terrible goings on. But never while I'm around. Such things never happen to me. Down deep, I know I'm only a kid, playing at this.

Most of us most of the time divide the world into two parts. On the one hand, there is the real and the significant and the vital; on the other hand there are our own affairs.

2

There is the field of action, and there are the sidelines where we sit, perhaps as confirmed spectators, more likely as bench-warmers, waiting for action. In newspapers, in novels and films, in history and biography, we see significant events proceeding with appropriate signs and wonders; we see meaning proclaimed; we see purposes articulated. This is the appeal of drama and literature, history and biography: the significance of significant events is made clear to us. Astronaut and detective hero, physician and scientist charm us and attract our envy with their self-confident participation. They know what they're doing and what they're doing seems to us especially real and potent. But we remain the readers and the spectators; it can't happen here. We turn our backs on the author or artist who dares to claim attention for the humdrum of ordinary lives such as ours, on the verge or on the spot, but without delineated significance. "Is not this the carpenter . . . here with us?" "Unless you see signs and wonders you will not believe."

The significant events of the world—and of God's dealing with it—move with signs and wonders. God's revelation, his grace, his judgment, his call—these things happen to people with an impact and with a flourish, with dramatic preparation and confirmation, with events recorded and significance delineated. So each of us feels. As for me, each of us tells himself, I hear about them in orderly and dramatic fashion from professors and books. There are notable and exciting and effective ministries in my time, and I can read of them. God may even be moving decisively with people down the hall or down the street, and this too I can observe. But for my own affairs, I am not part of any of this, not really and not yet. The daily affairs of *my* ministry are at least as unlikely raw material for significant involvement in God's work as the people of Nazareth found this carpenter's life. Although perhaps I am only a few steps from the pool, I am still not in it.

I know all about the dramatic possibilities of personal counseling, and I watch with fascination the reports of others who venture into this pool ahead of me and can report, in their case studies, some of the wonders of such intimate involvement and significant changes. But when that high school girl stops me in the hall Sunday evening with her half-disguised, badly articulated sense of personal difficulty, this isn't the same thing, or not the "real thing." It's not the time, it's not the place, it's not the way this dramatically effective counseling can go on. She's not able to articulate her problems clearly, to develop insight, to achieve rapport in the way that counselees in the case studies are. Most significantly, however, I'm just not ready. She ought to be able to see that I'm only wearing a kind of mask. I don't yet have the experience or the resources that make me the kind of minister she needs to bring God's healing. So, encounter with her is not a moment for immersion into the pool. She is to be dealt with kindly, perhaps desperately, perhaps helpfully, but without the conviction that this encounter is really a moment of the genuine and significant ministry which God intends and which I am waiting and watching for.

I know all the theories of the moods and rhythms of worship, how God reaches down and man reaches up and they meet with a spark of re-creation. But worship in the seminary—that was for hearing what professors or fellow students had to say or else something to contend about. And worship in my church—that is something to plan with the deacons about, to fret about late Saturday night, to spar with the organist about, to conduct with or without some pleasure and some confidence on Sunday morning. But it's always on the verge. That God should reach down and speak a radical and direct and personal word to me in the midst of Sunday morning worship—this is as remote and unlikely as the sick man ever getting into the pool. I—like him—know too well all the reasons it can't happen.

The full and responsible participation of my congregation in the community and world around them—this takes a sophisticated theological and sociological understanding of the issues, and this takes a concern and dedication—signs and wonders, which I and these people don't now have. Maybe sometime after this congregation grows into maturity, or maybe sometime in another congregation—maybe sometime I can get out of this carpenter's shop and into an effective ministry.

Some men can testify to a clear conviction of God's vocation for them, an unshakable confidence that he has called them and a sure knowledge of what he has called them to. And there may even have been moments in which each of us has momentarily experienced such conviction. But for the most part, we are still looking and searching—looking to find that clear sense of leading which can become the foundation for effective ministry. "I have no man to put me into the pool . . . I am just involved in my ordinary, undramatic groping and fumbling."

Most difficult and impossible of all is that acceptance of God and that faith in his acceptance that we talk so much about and which we have known momentarily from time to time. We are on the verge of this personal faith constantly, so close to it that we are experts in it. But that we should actually experience it, here and now in this hectic, transitional, mixed-up, humdrum kind of life that we now lead—what could be so fanciful as that idea? Someday the sense of God's presence and his call will be clear and convincing to us, but not yet.

Meanwhile, while we try to fill the many, large, and sometimes mysterious responsibilities of the ministry, we may feel more like a boy wearing his father's clothes, or imitating his father's voice on the telephone and hoping no one will notice.

Or as ministers trying to comprehend and engage the forces within and between persons, within the church, and within the society which the church must confront, we may sometimes feel like the small boy looking through the knothole of a fence while the big boys are smoking, or playing football, or talking about girls. Or maybe we are like the small boy who has brazenly climbed the fence and is trying to keep up with the big boys at their exploits. The small boy lives with feelings mixed between fear at having his brazenness and weakness uncovered and in the buoyant hope of eventually really deserving a place inside the fence among the big boys.

Or perhaps we sometimes feel more like the young adolescent, head over book, or walking home alone, overhearing the others tell of their exploits from last Saturday night or their plans for the next. "Someday maybe I, too, will be in, but now I wait on the outside, looking in and looking on." Or like the adolescent, when he does date, feels it as a time of learning how to get along with girls, of getting ready to have the kind of good times other people seem to be having naturally.

Or maybe, going through all the motions of ministry, we feel like a member of a college debating team, or the student government. We earnestly, maybe even feverishly, spend ourselves as in the debating and the politicking, maybe even win acclaim and success. But down deep, we know all along that we are not engaged with the "real world." We are practicing, developing skills, getting ready, waiting and watching for the "real" engagement which is to come.

These are analogies with experiences of earlier years. Perhaps for many of us, they are more than analogies, perhaps they are also history.

However long has been one's ministry, ten days, ten months, ten years, he may still feel like the man who moves into a new house or a new office and looks around making note of things *with respect to the future*. "That chair will be comfortable to sit in, as soon as I finish this paperwork that keeps me at the desk chair now. That window will be pleasant to read by when I start spending more time reading. That wall will be a good one for the two pictures I have in the attic. The neighbor seems pleasant; I'm going to enjoy getting acquainted with him." But all these experiences remain as future anticipations. We are still making these promises to ourselves until the day we move out. They never come to pass. So, too, with our anticipation of finding the clear word to speak, the steady discipline of time and mind, the patient calmness of personal empathy, the vital engagement of men's ardors and responsibilities.

Our sense of being on the sidelines, of being not yet engaged in the "real thing," always has this expectation of imminence along with it. We are not in the pool yet, but we *are* on the verge. All it takes now is someone to carry us into the pool. Next time may be it. Just a little more preparation and planning, just a slight change in the condition and circumstances, then all will be well. Each of us has his own way of promising himself that moments of significance, of faithfulness, of effectiveness are just ahead: Right now the circumstances aren't quite right; I'm too unprepared, too ordinary, too fumbling. Just a little more patching here and a little more polishing there, then I'll be in ministry. Then I'll be ready to say, "Come down, Lord." I'll just get my New Testament Greek a little better. I'll just get a little better acquainted in town. I'll just lay a little more foundation with the deacons. I'll just wait until the family isn't quite so demanding. I'll just wait until I can figure out a little better why some of these people hang back. I'll just wait until we get the budget up to where we can support a good program. I'll "begin" just as soon as I can have an assistant or some laymen to help me with some of this busy work. If the "real thing" can't happen here, it will happen just around the corner. If I'm not really active and engaged in it—well, I almost am. Carry me down into the pool, and I'll be healed. That's the kind of help the ill man and we look for.

But that is not how he was restored. *There is no such thing as being on the verge.* It only feels that way. Either be sick where you are, or else there, *where you are,* "Take up your pallet and walk." There is no moratorium possible. There is no exemption assigned. Wherever you are, however you are, you are living as fully in the world, you are exercising as complete a ministry as you ever will. People are

7

looking to you now (and perhaps away again), affected one way or another by what you say and do. And they won't come back again whenever you finally announce that you are "ready." For you never will. Our moments come and go and our actions and decisions in them, even in the most unlikely moments and the most unprepared states, affect us and others irrevocably.

For we are assured of two things. First, the future, the next stage and the next moment to which we may look with so much confidence, will turn out to be just as murky as our present state. That moment—getting married, raising the budget, getting to know the deacons, getting the children out of diapers—which we expect to provide the purifying baptism will instead only bring us new murkiness. It won't really change anything. We who are not prepared for the Lord and his call now and know we are not never will be prepared. That final purifying baptism in the pool is not to be ours.

Significant events never happen with the clarity and dramatic preparation which they come in retrospect to have in the writing of history and biography. What seems in the novel and the drama, in the history and the biography to be of such lucid significance, happens, if it happens at all, only in the midst of the most humdrum and ordinary and unlikely and unprepared moments. Only in retrospect do events yield their pattern and their significance.

For, second, we are assured that this present hectic, ordinary, unprepared life is not really ordinary and is not really unprepared. For God is here. We don't have to send pleadingly, "Come down, Lord." He is already here and working his healing to us and through us. We don't have to beg or wait or yearn for special baptism in the Bethesda pool. We have only to rise up *on the verge:*

"Take up your pallet."

We needn't despair of present humdrumness, hindrance, or hecticness. Nor must we hide in false hopes of the future, of another place or time where signs and wonders and certainty and readiness will abound. It is just possible that in the unlikeliness of your present situation and with all the unlikeliness of yourself as you now are, even in the routines of your life this day—not even waiting until your headache feels better or until you get those letters written, or until you get those phone calls made or until you get away from the phone, or until you have a chance to look up something in the reference book, or until you can consult about it or even make up your own mind—God may touch you to cleanse, to reveal, to chasten, to claim you and your ministry.

INTERLUDE

WHAT
THIS
BOOK
IS

This book is a meditation with ministers. I am asking to share some of whatever time they give—more usually in privacy without such intrusions—to their innermost reflections about themselves and their ministry. These are the moments away from the planning and decision-making about particular people and programs, when they reflect, perhaps gingerly, on these decisions and plannings and all their other labors, when they ask themselves how they are doing and what they are doing. How do these labors fit with the call and vision which started them? How do they now view their role and the way they are filling it? In these private moments of reflection, moods will range from exhilaration to despair. I am asking especially to share those moments when a minister feels, as a predicament and with some despair, that he and his ministry are "on the verge," in the way I have just described. It is only one of many ways a man may feel about his ministry. Perhaps this mood may often be held simultaneously with others. But I suppose I think it is a common experience, or I would not be writing about it.

I try to describe this predicament and thus evoke and objectify it and make it more readily available for a minister to reflect on it. I also try to address this predicament with insights from varying perspectives, perhaps some of the same insights which the minister may be making himself, perhaps some that complement his. My attempts at "insight" come from a range of perspectives, most recognizably, perhaps, perspectives that can be called psychological and theological. The modes of address vary too. The earlier chapters are the more frankly "meditative." These are intended to be in the language, including scriptural, with which a minister may most naturally think about his own experience. The psychological and theological perspectives are there but are not bared. Later chapters make these perspectives more explicit in more "analytic" less "existential" mode. I suspect that the earlier chapters will "ring true" more than the later ones, which move away from the experience and attempt to probe into what lies "behind" or "within" it. It may be that they *are* truer, and that different lines of analysis in the later chapters would be more accurate. But I have—as I invite ministers to do—ventured to invest myself in my particular line of analysis just as fully, yet freely, as I can. I know that it would be safer, and in some important sense, truer, to stay with the scriptural generalities of the opening sections. But these generalities lodge in particulars and details of experience and can be fully known—as well as obscured—by the analysis of those particulars. I risk obscuring in the hope of greater illumination. And I fully expect both—just as this paragraph, attempting analysis of the rationale for the book, must both obscure and clarify.

One form of expressing the clergyman's dilemma these days is in the poignant concern for relevance, the need to be where the action is. Perhaps this book would be more relevant, would be less "on the verge" if it would discuss the issue of relevance more directly. But I think the question of relevance is only a form of a more long-standing, persistent, and fundamental predicament faced by ministers. It is also my hunch that, common as is the word "relevance" in public discussion, ministers are more likely to think to themselves about their predicament in the more general terms I have used in this book. I realize that not to enter more directly and vigorously the debate over relevance runs the risk of suffering precisely the withdrawal and aloofness the book is about. And the decision is made, as is often the case with the minister, regretfully and wistfully. But I think, also as is often the case with the minister, it is the proper decision, for it avoids what I think in this case

11

would be the still more perilous danger, what is called in the closing chapters a "hot" bondage.

Another and related form of the discussion in our time uses the language of secularism and makes its critique of the "forms" of religion. Bultmann, Brunner, Barth, Bonhoeffer, Gogarten, Tillich, and the Niebuhrs, not to mention the flashier American and British statements of secularism and reform in the 60's, each raises—and appropriately so—serious questions about the validity and faithfulness of the institutions and forms and language which claim to represent the Christian faith. When they recommend one or another "secular" expressions as more faithful, they run the risk of what will be called later "hot" bondage, sometimes forgetting that their recommended expressions are only particular forms, at least as likely to be limited and ambiguous as those they would replace When they rebuke the religious forms in the name of the absolutes and ultimates which provide the criterion, they risk the "cool" bondage to which this book is mostly addressed, the aloof withdrawal from any particular and actual involvement, forgetting in their passion for purity of faith, that man must live in the world of particular forms, not among the absolutes. When they—as all do in one way or another, and perhaps especially the Niebuhrs— urge men to penitent investment of themselves in the forms of our day, simultaneously celebrating the faithfulness and confessing the faithlessness of the forms, then they provide a major perspective to which this book, in its own ambiguous way, tries to give expression.

WRITING A BOOK IS RISKY INVESTMENT

I would rather have started the above section with: "This book is a meditation with Christians." I don't really want to write just to professional clergymen about dilemmas in their professional life. I want to write about—and think the book really is about—the nature of the Christian life, and the dilemmas in it.

I want to write particularly about the dilemma of trying to live responsibly in the two worlds in which a Christian finds himself, that world of ultimate claims and assurances in which the Christian occasionally feels himself belonging (or occasionally wants to), and that overwhelmingly immediate everyday world of people and things in which he knows he is unmistakably immersed. The Christian's predicament is that he knows they are both God's worlds and are not really two worlds at all, but he feels the disparity between them keenly and utterly.

I want to write about the temptation to abandon one of these worlds for the sake of the other. I want to write especially about the agonies of finding oneself holding out on the immediate everyday world, held back, in part, by allegiance to those important ultimates which seem to be contradicted by the immediate particulars. (I think that most people likely to pick up this book already recognize too keenly to need further reminder from me, the other dilemma, the risk of abandoning loyalty to the ultimates for the sake of wholehearted participation in the immediate.)

I also want to write about the drama and exhilaration of living in both worlds with the freedom to which we have come to give the special name "Christian freedom," of participating fully and devotedly in the immediate particulars at the same time that one is fully aware that they are not the same as the ultimates, cannot command or deserve ultimate loyalty, and need correction from the ultimates.

I want to write about these "dynamics" of the Christian life.

But in an important sense there is no such thing as "the Christian life." That is only an abstraction, real but an abstraction. There are only Christian lives. There are only—for such purposes as this, at least—particular people making particular decisions about particular alternatives, experiencing particular events, relationships, and feelings. This poses a problem for me just like the one I want to write about. I can write about the abstractions, as I have in the paragraph above, and they may have a certain reality and vigor for some readers in some respects. But this is not likely to engage or illuminate very vitally anyone at the existential, concrete point at which he feels these matters. I can stick to particulars and narrate events, as in biography or autobiography. But then I lose the very analytic and illuminative power that derives from the perspective beyond the events. To work with abstractions is to risk losing vitality. To work with concrete instances is to risk losing power and generality. The writer's dilemma is not unlike the Christian's, and perhaps most writers, at least of books of this kind, choose the same horns and same risks that this book contends most Christians do: they prefer to preserve their fidelity to the abstract truth and to risk losing the vitality that might come with more concrete involvement.

But writer or Christian has the prospect of investing himself into particular expressions and forms, fully aware that these are not to be identified with the ultimates and the abstractions which transcend them, but also knowing that he is not likely to engage these ultimates except as he finds them in the concrete particulars. And with this knowledge comes (1) the freedom to address the particulars vigorously and unreservedly, because he can see them for what they are (as good an instance as he will ever find of the grander abstractions with which he is concerned), but also (2) the freedom to address them with a playfulness and a lightness that comes from seeing them for what they are (only particular and transient expressions).

I shall be writing about particular vocational dilemmas of the parish minister. Here are particular types of dilemmas which I think I know well and to which I think I can bring helpfully to bear these more general perspectives. The risks are great. There is the risk of feeding the already too popular stereotype that the professional clergyman is the epitome of the religious man. There is the risk of missing many readers whom I might want to try to reach. There is the risk of becoming so embroiled and bogged down in the particular professional problems of ministry (just as the preceding paragraphs have become too much bogged down in the problems of the writer) so as to lose sight of the principal point. But the risks of not going out on a limb, of not trying to address a particular problem, are greater. The risks of holding back for the sake of purity and ideal loyalty to the most ultimate values, are the risks of saying and doing nothing.

It is primarily to this fear of investment that the book is addressed. And its first address is to make the risky investment. To struggle with the professional problems of the parish minister may not be at the center of what it means to live the Christian life.

14

A book which devotes its longest chapters to questions of preaching and parish administration may be very much at the disappointing periphery of what either writer or reader would like to think of as central questions. But the central questions may elude us indefinitely if we do not take what we find on the verge.

MINISTRY
IS ALWAYS
IN THE
INTERIM

> For it will be as when a man going on a journey called his servants and entrusted to them his property; to one he gave five talents, to another two, to another one, to each according to his ability. Then he went away.
>
> *Matthew 25:14–15*

The master is away and the servants are on their own—with the master's goods. The master is coming back and his return promises a dire moment of accountability for the servants.

The minister knows this plight. He feels himself charged with responsibilities fraught with life and death consequences. God's church and the souls of his people are in his care. But he also feels himself—at least for the time being—in a helpless, unprepared interim. He neither feels mastery over these matters nor knows the master's guiding presence. He is on his own, but what he does has consequences disproportionate to his own resources. The minister knows this plight—whether or not he adds to it the consternation of feeling himself a man of one talent, envious of those with five. The minister knows more than a little of those ambiguous circumstances referred to by this parable, the unclear demanding time between call and fulfillment, between commitment and consummation, between enlistment in the service of the master and the searing experience of becoming wholly his, that time marked traditionally between his first and second comings.

In Matthew, the parable is, almost unavoidably, immediately preceded by that of the virgins and the lamps, with its message of watchful waiting for the master—"You know neither the day nor the hour"—and is immediately followed by the vision of the last judgment in which the judged are astounded that they have encountered the master in the needy stranger even while they watched and waited for the more glorious consummation. Luke insists more explicitly that the parable refers to the particular dilemmas of living in the interim. The parable gives us Jesus' final words before going up to Jerusalem, and all that implies about the master leaving, and coming again. He told it, Luke says (Luke 19:11) "because he was near to Jerusalem and because they supposed that the kingdom of God was to appear immediately."

How is life to be lived in that undefined but breathlessly expectant time after the master has gone and before he returns in fulfillment? In suspension of those ordinary and tainted matters which occupy importance in the world before it is touched and transformed by the master? Should the servant just bury his money? Or only in fervent preparation? Is the servant to be governing all by his anticipation of the dramatic moment to come when the period of waiting is over? Surely this breathless time is not to be spent in concern for such unexalted worldly matters as providing oil for lamps and investing money and attending to the worldly needs of unpleasant strangers—as though these had some relation to the dramatic completion to come? Yet it may be so.

How is one to conduct himself in that anticlimactic time after he knows himself justified and is living in expectation of fulfillment, that period of being yet becoming a man of faith, that period of knowing oneself saved, yet still tainted. With reckless heedlessness of the concerns and needs of the world, including those petty concerns for right and wrong, good and bad, and for human sanctions which may once have immobilized him and from which he now feels liberated? If scrupulosity is required, it must be in preparation for affairs of the world to come. Surely the justified man is not asked to give scrupulous attention to the trivial affairs and daily encounters of his former world as though they bore the import of the world to come. Yet it may be so.

How is one to live after he has felt himself called to a ministry of healing and transformation of the world, yet is still awaiting the fulfillment of that call which will render him able to achieve that healing and transformation? This is that interim of being called but unprepared, called but not yet suitably placed, called but dealing with people not yet trained to be responsive to one's ministry—called but slashing through a jungle of organizational barriers to a moment of real ministry, called but only tentatively called and not so sure yet of the call as to act on it.

This is the interim which starts out to be the student moratorium years of preparation, then extends into the first assignment, then the second, as these still seem to be times of preparation and apprenticeship, as work in these assignments is defined and sustained by anticipation of the rich effective ministry yet to come. It is the interim of anticipation which finally becomes the bittersweet daydream of what might have been.

How is one to be a minister when he feels not yet a minister, while he waits for the times to ripen and himself to mature? By renouncing those vestigial ligaments that bind him to that world he is called to transform: the trivialities, the banalities, the meaninglessnesses, the groping inarticulateness, the unruliness, the petty antagonisms and self-seeking, the complacencies, the blind and mechanical conventionalities, the lamp to be tended, the money to be counted and invested, the inconveniently fallen stranger (or is he an unready churchman?), awkwardly blocking the path toward ministry? Are we to withhold ourselves in miserly preparation for the genuine ministry yet to come, when times will change?

Surely each of the trivial occasions and encounters of the present—those phone calls and committee meetings, that insufferable Council of Churches' president, those unruly kids and that scripturally illiterate congregation, the woman threatening suicide, the man threatening divorce, and the deacon threatening resignation, and all the other harassments against which one feels helpless—surely these unlikely occasions are not to be taken seriously, for their own sake, as though genuine ministry can take place in them. Yet it may be so.

Entering the ministry has been likened * to joining the army precisely because of this paradox of earnest commitment and uncertainty over its expression. The recruit enlists in the army with a determination of purpose possibly even well defined, yet he typically has little idea how and when and where and by what means and with whom he will serve. And more likely than not the dramatic and glorious moment he anticipated when he enlisted never comes, and he must reconcile his sense of purpose somehow with the drudgeries of army routines.

Perhaps a more effective analogy is that of engagement for marriage. Here too is interim between commitment and anticipated fulfillment. The couple lives between the relationship of dating which they have left behind and the relationship of marriage to which their present status is pointing. They are committed to the more permanent, more binding, more intimate, and deeper relationship of marriage, yet they must find and express that relationship without the opportunities and occasions which marriage will provide. Are

---

* William Adams Brown, Mark A. May, and Frank K. Shuttleworth, *The Education of American Ministers*, Vol. II, *The Profession of the Ministry: Its Status and Problems* (New York: Institute of Social and Religious Research, 1934).

they to renounce the dances, the double dating, the phone calls and all the other patterns of the dating relationship because these seem to represent what they are leaving behind as less mature? Are they, instead, to constrict their relation to one of relentless planning for the ceremony, home, and furniture of the future? Or is there some way by which the relationship of the anticipated and committed future is somehow expressed with the ordinary materials of the present which one is tempted to relegate to the past? For if the couple does not find deepening intimacy and affection even in the paradoxical interim of engagement, they are not likely to find it in the anticipated moments of marriage either; these will turn out to be ordinary occasions, too, not glamorously fulfilling, and they will become but continuing preparation and anticipation, an interim waiting for fulfillment.

So the minister's dilemma is to express a ministry with resources and activities and organizations and people and circumstances that seem quite unsuitable and unready for the nature of the ministry as it ought to be and, as the minister may like to think, it someday will be for him. That holy work which somehow seems more properly to belong still in one's future must somehow be undertaken with the very worldly raw materials of one's present. But this paradoxical guideline itself may seem another one of those counsels of perfection which can be thought of, if at all, only in terms of some future realization.

Meanwhile, one seems more likely to fall off on one side or the other. He may immerse himself—and lose himself—in the trivialities and banalities and secularities of the present worldly life—whether in suburb or inner city, country club or city hall, office routines of the study or of the denominational headquarters. He may celebrate these, and forget the vision of the demanding glorious ministry to which he once felt called. About this peril we are not now speaking. Or he may renounce the insufficient raw materials and resources of the present and live only in determined preparation for that which is to come. In extreme forms, this produces one or more forms of asceticism and cavalier disregard for the people and things of this world. It is about the more subtle forms of this peril that we speak here.

One approaches his ministry with the conviction that the gospel *will* be proclaimed vigorously, human relationships *will* be healed, people *will* be aroused to mission. But these attainments are awaiting, if not the master's return, then at least some convincingly propitious signs that the times are more ripe than the present interim moment. Full investment of self and talent await clearer direction and more certain promise of return. I will throw myself into disciplined preparation and vigorous delivery of sermons as soon as I have more evidence that the congregation can benefit from the extra effort and investment. That brilliant insight into the world situation needs to be developed into an article for *The Christian Century* or into a guest lecture they may ask for back at the seminary, or into a letter to Professor Brown, but not squandered on the old lady I'm driving to see. I'll be glad to work hard on the committee for ecumenical relations or for raising money for the ghetto program, but I'll work harder if it has some of the important ministers on it and gets plenty of newspaper publicity or shows some of the other signs that this is an occasion of fruition. I'll speak if it's long distance calling, or if the stipend is great enough, or if there is other evidence that this is the real thing the Master wants me to do. Otherwise, I'll bury my talent and wait for the right times.

Is it that we feel too good to be true to the calling that comes in the interim moment? Do these callings of the past and the vision of the fulfillment to come stand out so gloriously that the present moment becomes too dreary? Or is it that we feel too unsure of ourselves to venture without the massive affirmation provided by the master's presence, or some comparable assurance. Do we mistrust the unlikely present occasions as interim times to pass over and do we look for impressive signs because we want these signs to match an exalted view of ourselves, or because we want them to compensate for a mistrustful view of self and call?

In either case, the answer is the same. Whether in rebuke or reassurance, we can be sure that the present moments and unlikely occasions are no less the Master's just because they lack the obvious signs of his grandeur. The present time and talents and tasks are his. We presume to judge occasions with a careful calculus, measuring need and worth and return as a way to determine the size of our investment. But this is not the Lord's way. He comes with overflowing abandon. He who gathers where he does not sow equally often sows where he cannot count on gathering. The time we count on to change things will not do so, and future time will turn out to be no more—but also, no less—glorious than the unseemly and incomplete time of waiting in which we find ourselves. For the God who made himself incarnate in the most unlikely of places and times stands ready to infuse with meaning and demand even the unlikely material of our daily lives.

WHO
AM I
THAT I
SHOULD
GO?

Now Moses was keeping the flock of his father-in-law, Jethro, the priest of Midian; and he led his flock to the west side of the wilderness, and came to Horeb, the mountain of God. And the angel of the Lord appeared to him in a flame of fire out of the midst of a bush; and he looked, and lo, the bush was burning, yet it was not consumed. And Moses said, "I will turn aside and see this great sight, why the bush is not burnt." When the Lord saw that he turned aside to see, God called to him out of the bush, "Moses, Moses!" And he said, "Here am I." Then he said, "Do not come near; put off your shoes from your feet, for the place on which you are standing is holy ground." And he said, "I am the God of your father, the God of Abraham, the God of Isaac, and the God of Jacob." And Moses hid his face, for he was afraid to look at God.

Exodus 3:1–6

"Come, I will send you to Pharaoh that you may bring forth my people, the sons of Israel, out of Egypt." But Moses said to God, "Who am I that I should go to Pharaoh, and bring the sons of Israel out of Egypt?" He said, "But I will be with you; and this shall be the sign for you, that I have sent you: when you have brought forth the people out of Egypt, you shall serve God upon this mountain."

Then Moses said to God, "If I come to the people of Israel and say to them, 'The God of your fathers has sent me to you,' and they ask me, 'What is his name?' what shall I say to them?" God said to Moses, "I AM WHO I AM." And he said, "Say this to the people of Israel, 'I AM has sent me to you.'"

Exodus 3:10–14

Then Moses answered, "But behold, they will not believe me or listen to my voice, for they will say, 'The Lord did not appear to you.'" The Lord said to him, "What is that in your hand?" He said, "A rod." And he said, "Cast it on the ground." So he cast it on the ground, and it became a serpent; and Moses fled from it. But the Lord said to Moses, "Put out your hand, and take it by the tail"—so he put out his hand and caught it, and it became a rod in his hand—"that they may believe that the Lord, the God of their fathers, the God of Abraham, the God of Isaac, and the God of Jacob, has appeared to you."

Exodus 4:1–5

But Moses said to the Lord, "Oh, my Lord, I am not eloquent, either heretofore or since thou hast spoken to thy servant; but I am slow of speech and of tongue." Then the Lord said to him, "Who has made man's mouth? Who makes him dumb, or deaf, or seeing, or blind? Is it not I, the Lord? Now therefore go, and I will be with your mouth and teach you what you shall speak." But he said, "Oh, my Lord, send, I pray, some other person."

Exodus 4:10–13

If we are trapped on the verge by the illusion that circumstances are not ready, we are equally often sidelined by the illusion that we ourselves are not ready. Perhaps daily encounters may seem too trivial and too unworthy of the glorious mission to which we have been called. So we wait for these daily trivia to pass away and for those circumstances to emerge which will call for true ministry. This is the form of interim-mentality just discussed. But daily encounters may sometimes seem too dramatic, too demanding, too awesome. Then we defer ministry until we (not the circumstances) improve and become worthy to exercise true ministry.

Ministers are accustomed to hearing laymen make their excuses: "I can't say the blessing at the church dinner, or call on new people in town for the church, or stand up and say my piece at the school board hearing. Who am I? I don't know what to say. No one will listen to me. Somebody else better do it. That's what you ministers are good at." *

A minister may equally often confess to his laymen his own sense of unreadiness, perhaps even timidity: "They didn't really train me for this kind of thing in seminary. . . . I don't think I'm the kind of person who does this most effectively." Together, laymen and minister may admire and envy the heroes of the faith, the competence, confidence, and conviction boldly displayed by the nineteenth-century pioneer missionaries, the Pilgrim forefathers, the Reformers, the early fathers, the disciples, the Old Testament prophets —back to that figure who must surely be the most stalwart apostle of either testament, Moses himself.

But we forget the feebleness felt by these champions of faith. How did Moses answer his call from God? The words sound familiar. "Who am I that I should go? . . . What shall I say? . . . They will not believe me or listen to my

---

* Sometimes, over-impressed by his own unique clerical capacities, a minister may take these excuses at face value, feed the resistance they represent, and engage in a training program to give the laymen the words and poise and polish he thinks they need to do these things; i.e., he tries to clericalize them. But this overcelebration of a minister's personal and professional readiness for ministry is what we considered in the last chapter and does not beset all ministers all the time.

voice. . . . I am not eloquent. . . . Oh, my Lord, send, I pray, some other person" (Exod. 3:11, 13; 4:1, 10, 13). Of course, Moses was taken by surprise by this unexpected summons. Maybe if he had had a little more notice, a little more time to prepare, a chance to fit it into his thinking and his schedule, maybe if he, like the stalwart religious man walking up the Jericho road past the fallen traveler, hadn't been preoccupied with other demands, maybe if he could have had a few courses, or a chance to "talk it over with someone," maybe a short in-palace training program on ministry to Pharaohs—then maybe he could have responded more positively, with, as we say these days, less "role-conflict" or less "passive-dependency."

But Moses *was* taken by surprise. He had left Egypt where the important action was, and was tending sheep in the wilderness. That is hardly a place where you expect to find the Lord, especially if you are in Moses' position and haven't read past Exodus to know how often that is just exactly where he and occasion for his ministry are found, in the ordinary and remote and unexpected and lowly, among people going about their daily affairs. The Lord seldom appears or summons in those occasions for which we are so carefully and confidently prepared. And when we are taken by surprise, Moses speaks for all of us in making excuses and stalling for time, and for a greater sense of confidence and competence. "Who am I that I should go? . . . What shall I say? . . . They will not believe me or listen to my voice. . . . I am not eloquent. . . . Oh, my Lord, send, I pray, some other person." "Call me next week, or next year, but I can't see my way clear to it this time." Meanwhile, on the verge—for a lifetime.

Perhaps you are ready to discuss the redemptive actions of God with confidence, perhaps even with brilliance, in the sermon or study group for which you have prepared. Perhaps you have learned how to "do" pastoral counseling, at its regularly appointed time and places, in the fifty minutes of standardized give and take. Perhaps, given time to reflect on others' discussion, you come up with helpful suggestions on social action, at the Council of Churches committee meeting.

But then there are those burning bushes which compel you to turn aside from the familiar path. They so often come in the wilderness, just when you leave the busy action in Egypt. Your seat partner on the plane discovers you are a minister and suddenly takes this so seriously that he pours out the pent-up question: What must I do to be saved? On vacation, you are suddenly ushered to the side of a dying man because he wants a minister and you're the only one around. Then his widow turns to you. You are finally locking the parish house Sunday evening after a long day, and there in the shadows of the front steps is a high school girl waiting to pour out her turbulent confessions. A neighborhood is caught up in a swirling and bitter crisis, and there you are in it—just where you should be able to relax. What started out as a routine welcoming call on new residents soon exposes bitter rancor in the family, with man and woman snapping at each other and asking, almost explicitly, for pastoral mediation. Then there is the sneering adolescent boy you encounter on what started out to be an informational guided tour of the detention home or the man who wants to know, after your carefully balanced statement from the pulpit, how you really think he should vote in the coming election.

These are the burning bushes so intense we, too, turn our faces away—not nearly so much in cowardice, as in honest recognition of the stark limitations of our puny resources. "Who am I that I should presume to meet this call?" "I just prayed I would have it in me." "I felt like an impostor. They were looking to me and really expecting me to do something about it." "Oh, my Lord, send, I pray, some other person." "It's a good thing I'm still in training (or still in my first pastorate) (or have signed up for the summer refresher course). When I get to be a real minister I can handle things like this." "It's a good thing I know a psychiatrist who does know how to handle these things (or a social worker, or psychologist, or a senior minister . . .)." "I should write the seminaries that they should have a course on *this* kind of problem, because I feel so unprepared for it."

So we live in a moratorium or exile of our own making, a kind of deferment—we refuse to say "exemption" for we see it as only temporary—from full ministry. This interim mood is compounded of despair, of hope in its overcoming, and a kind of scramble to hasten the overcoming.

But this scurrying for assurance only leads us farther into the wilderness, the wilderness of contrived evidence of assurance, the wilderness of those signs and wonders which lead us away from, rather than toward, what they would point to. Moses asked for concrete evidence of his authority and God's support, and he got instead, a rod full of magic powers. The Jewish people later succumbed to the same temptation and built for themselves a golden calf. Then they built an ark and a temple and an intricate legal system to contain this awesome God of the burning bush and to make him manageable. For ministers, the assuring evidence of readiness for ministry may be sought in the signs and wonders of professionalism, of smoothness and poise, of a battery of techniques, of well-defined roles, or else in the signs and wonders of concrete results to be tallied, people and dollars to be counted. But this search for assurance, before we start, leads us further into the wilderness because we become so burdened down with the tools and armor and badges of merit that we lose our way and forget what we were about.

"Who am I that I should go?"

The Lord's answer to Moses: "But I will be with you."

This is, first of all, a rebuke. Who are you to be saying, "Who am I?" You may have problems about identity or many other things. But this has nothing to do with whether you should go. It has nothing to do with whether your mission will be effective. Take off your shoes. You are standing on holy ground. Take off the anxiety and fussing you usually wear and enjoy as part of yourself. This is different from your usual worries about achieving and about pleasing other people. This is the Lord who is calling you and who is with you. Of course, it is natural to be concerned about establishing rapport with the seat partner, the high school girl, the bickering family, and all the rest, to be worried about gaining their acceptance, and to be showing a congenial "acceptance" toward them. Of course, it is natural to be concerned about one's own self-acceptance, to be able to leave one of these encounters and feel the satisfaction of having done something helpful (or at least of having done something right—those seminary professors may still be lurking over your shoulder). But don't be so presumptuous as to confuse these natural but personal concerns with the question of God's acceptance of you or of another, or with the question of the achievement of God's purposes. God has little need of these personal relationships or personal satisfactions, which we have so much need of. They hardly provide reliable indices of the presence of God or of the accomplishment of his purposes. This is the grossest kind of anthropomorphism, to project upon God the face of those parents, professors, parishioners, or others whose approval and praise is important.

If I pray that I may have it in me to serve, my prayer is an offense: I betray my concern to justify myself. If I feel like an impostor, I am—not because my resources are so feeble but because the pretentions betrayed by this feeling are so high. Where do I get the idea that I am looked to to be more than I am? It is illusion and pretention to suppose that we will ever be more ready than we are now, that our faith will ever be surer, our vocation clearer, our competence more established (just as it is an illusion to wait for the circumstances to be more glorious or propitious than now). Our limitations as human servants to the living God are far more radical and essential than we so glibly claim when we say, "Wait until next year." Christ sent his disciples forth with nothing but the promise that "it shall be given you . . . what ye shall speak" (Matt. 10, KJV). Do you really think

29

that *you* are going to do any healing of persons or peoples—now or in the future?

"I will be with you" is a rebuke also because it reminds us that we refuse to take the Lord's call as seriously and urgently as he does. The Lord calls us now because he needs us now. Another turns to us now because he needs us now. We are summoned, like Moses, to release someone from bondage now. But we say "not yet"—while men stay in bondage and death. We go through the proper motions of involvement, anxious all the while that we are not prepared for it and accordingly stay safely aloof from that total involvement which ministry would require. From our own anxious perspective, we keep our fingers crossed, feeling "this one doesn't count." But how fearfully this one does count, for another and in the eyes of God. This occasion for ministry will not come again.

The unlikely carpenter from Nazareth read from the scripture of the release of the captive and dared to say, "This day the scripture is fulfilled." It is not *self*-confidence that breathes such claims of immediacy but an atunement to the movements of God and his unlikely comings.

For "I will be with you" is stern rebuke only because it is faithful promise, a promise known by every man who has ventured into the wilderness at God's bidding, not knowing where he was going.

"I stayed by the dying man, not knowing what to do, so I just held his hand. He opened his eyes and smiled and whispered 'Good-bye' and died."

"I walked the streets of the impossible neighborhood, my head hanging from the misery of not knowing what to do. Then a man stopped me and said, 'I want to talk to you, Father . . .'"

"When the fellow began talking to me on the plane I realized this was only a one-hour conversation. There weren't going to be any repercussions, pro or con, from whatever I did. I wasn't trying to get or keep anybody in the church. He didn't even know my name. Those things I usually fret about secretly didn't count on this one. So I wasn't trying hard to do the 'right' thing. I just tried to understand what he was trying to say. Imagine my surprise when he said at the end that this was the turning point of his life."

"When I saw that girl that night I was so tired I couldn't think of theology or ethics or counseling or anything else. I just said, 'Let's go someplace where we can relax.' So we went to the back of the bowling alley and I sat there with my shoes off (pretending I was changing into bowling shoes). I don't really know what we talked about. I think I probably talked as much about myself as she did about herself. But when it was all over, it seemed the most real thing that happened to me that day."

ADVENT
ACCORDING
TO
MARK

If call to ministry is ambiguous, even terrifying, and leaves one yearning for more direct assurance and guidance at the moment of action, perhaps we can find this direction in the rhythms of encounter provided by seasons of the church year. Advent, for example, is to provide the impetus for the renewal of another season of faith. But Advent is an ironically treacherous way to begin a church year, at least as we select our celebration of Christmas from Matthew and from Luke. It is probably fortunate that our seasons have shifted so that Advent does not really coincide for us with the beginning of much in church or ministry except the fiscal year. The church year really begins in the fall, as my desk calendar, prepared for ministers, testifies. And commencements and ordinations are in the spring, all safely away from the temptations of taking keynote from our Christmas imagery. So long as Christmas means angels and gentle shepherds and adoring animals and wise men, we perhaps do best to leave it to children and to stores. For we are already sorely tempted to make this sentimental, pacific mood the norm for church and ministry.

We are so accustomed to understanding the Advent of our Lord with the stories told by Matthew and Luke, with an occasional reference to the metaphysics of John 1, that we are startled to consider the possibility that Mark, too, has a version of how Christ comes to men. Yet the church has found Advent lessons in Mark. Here is one of them, neither sentimental nor metaphysical, but chaotic and turbulent, not a proper beginning at all, but smack in the middle of things:

Jesus went away to the lake-side with his disciples. Great numbers from Galilee, Judaea and Jerusalem, Idumaea and Transjordan, and the neighbourhood of Tyre and Sidon, heard what he was doing and came to see him. So he told his disciples to have a boat ready for him, to save him from being crushed by the crowd. For he cured so many that sick people of all kinds came crowding in upon him to touch him. The unclean spirits too, when they saw him, would fall at his feet and cry aloud, "You are the Son of God"; but he insisted that they should not make him known.

He then went up into the hill-country and called the men he wanted; and they went and joined him. He appointed twelve as his companions, whom he would send out to proclaim the Gospel, with a commission to drive out devils. So he appointed the Twelve: to Simon he gave the name Peter; then came the sons of Zebedee, James and his brother John, to whom he gave the name Boanerges, Sons of Thunder; then Andrew and Philip and Bartholomew and Matthew and Thomas and James the son of Alphaeus and Thaddaeus and Simon, a member of the Zealot party, and Judas Iscariot, the man who betrayed him.

He entered a house; and once more such a crowd collected round them that they had no chance to eat. When his family heard of this, they set out to take charge of him; for they were saying that he was out of his mind.

The doctors of the law, too, who had come down from Jerusalem, said, "He is possessed by Beelzebub," and, "He drives out devils by the prince of devils." So he called them to come forward, and spoke to them in parables: "How can Satan drive out Satan? If a kingdom is divided against itself, that kingdom cannot stand; if a household is divided against itself, that house will never stand; and if

Satan is in rebellion against himself, he is divided and cannot stand; and that is the end of him.

"On the other hand, no one can break into a strong man's house and make off with his goods unless he has first tied the strong man up; then he can ransack the house."

Mark 3:7–27, NEB

What a chaotic passage. The scene shifts without reason or pattern from seaside to hills to village. Jesus is represented both as wanting to escape the press of the crowd and as welcoming it. Two remarks of Jesus' are inconceivably juxtaposed: One gives a straight-faced account of a primitive mind conducting conversation with demons; the other has him devastating the scribes with a witheringly sophisticated argument. But the argument is called a "parable" and seems almost a conundrum in which Jesus is somehow identified with Satan, and God is a plunderer. No wonder modern commentators—the scribes of our day—give us little but reconstruction, telling us how this passage must be rewritten to make sense. It's too bad the early compilers were not such clever men and left the passage so confused. Matthew and Luke did a little better in using the scene as the occasion for an orderly sermon.

But the chaos of the passage is nothing compared with the chaos of the scenes it portrays: turbulent clamoring mobs; afflicted, festering, demented; pushing Jesus into the sea; crowding into the house; while Jesus somehow (perturbed or unruffled, we do not know) preaches, heals, holds virtually simultaneous conversation with demons, with scribes, and with a solicitous family—and incidentally commissions his disciples. Indeed, commissioning in the midst of such hubbub, without such amenities as the all-night prayer Luke has preceding the call to the disciples or the instructions Matthew has him giving the disciples after they have been called. No wonder Jesus' family thought he was out of his mind. The scribes' diagnosis might have been the kinder one, only that he was possessed by Beelzebub.

What kind of Advent lesson is this, to suggest that Christ comes into the lives of the people with neither fanfare nor calm, with neither unassailable vigor nor overwhelming purity? If this chaos is the best Mark can do to tell us a Christmas story, what a blessing that Matthew and Luke could make up the deficiency and tell us the real Christmas story, where everything blossoms out clear, calm, and—why not say it in a book celebrating risky venture—stable! We much prefer the real Christmas stories of Matthew and Luke. We regard the nomination of such a passage from Mark as a sham, or at best, a makeshift substitute foisted on us by a church arbitrarily or politically trying to find something from each Gospel for each season.

There is for us too, a real church and a real ministry in which angels and shepherds and wise men and holy families all play their appointed roles with serenity and order and virtue and confidence. There is also another ministry which is disordered and chaotic and fragmented and unfulfilled, in the midst of pressing, afflicted crowds, in which a minister, too, feels out of his mind and possessed. This rugged Markan version of ministry may be much more believable. We may know it much more intimately than the idealized idyll. But it still somehow seems to us sham and makeshift substitute compelled by arbitrary exigencies. We long for the real ministry of the ideal and idyll—idol and idle though it may be.

The "real" Christmas story, and the "real" church and ministry are there firmly in our memories and in our anticipations—those stable times of the past and of the future in which there is no problem in knowing what the church is or what a Christian does and believes. At one time in the past, when we knew the real Christmas and the real church, it was like this: what you had to do was to hold still during the pageant, if you were Joseph, or keep in step, if you were the wise men, speak out loud enough to be heard in the back of the room, don't whisper to each other, and come to rehearsal on time. The church was easy to recognize: it consisted of the ladies who fussed to get you in costume, and the men who set up the mike for the pageant, and the people who told you afterward how well you had done. The mission of the church was clear in those days too. A Negro minister appeared in the pulpit every year on Race Relation Sunday in February. At Thanksgiving time, you brought in cans of food for the people in the old folks home somewhere just outside of town; and at Christmastime you filed past the chancel and laid an envelope of money in the manger, money which was to be used for something called "paying off the mortgage." There wasn't any problem in the former times in identifying and following the real ministry. And there won't be any problem in the future, either, identifying the church and its ministry. The church will be that gathered group of earnest, informed, and committed believers and activists who are responsive to your leadership. But meanwhile, in the in-between times, things are a little more hectic and less stable. Things meanwhile are more like the crude, primitive chaotic account of Mark. And the church which asks us to read this account in Advent has the boldness to suggest that Christ and his ministry can enter such chaotic lives in such a chaotic fashion. Mark doesn't know these "real" Christmas stories which tell of the coming of Jesus in the midst of pastoral and angelic scenes and the message of peace. Mark's story begins with a wild man in the wilderness and ends with three terrified women fleeing from a grave. Jesus first appears in this Gospel in the chaos of the wilderness, and his last words are his cry of despair from the cross, "My God, my God, why hast thou forsaken me?" (*Mark 15:34*, KJV)

And Mark speaks in the passage at hand of an itinerant preacher with hardly a stable institutional base or constituency—even as you and I find our ministry. He speaks of a man, held victim by the pressure of crowds—even as you and I find our ministry. He speaks of a man of vision whose expression is curtailed by authorities—even as you and I find our ministry. He speaks of Jesus hampered as much by family and friends as by foes—even as you and I find our ministry. He speaks of men being called to a task—even as you and I find our ministry—with something less than clear job specifications or role definition, and with something less than unambiguous loyalty to or acquaintance with the one who calls them.

According to Mark, the only ones in this episode who recognize Jesus for what he is are the mobs and the demons. His family and the religious authorities have no ears to hear.

Jesus' final words in this passage *may* be a logical counter-attack to the scribes at their own logic-chopping level. But if these words are the parable Mark says they are, they seem to be telling us that kingdom comes precisely to a divided house and to a strong man bound.

In all this Mark assaults our yearning for stability and order and peace as the signs of the kingdom with an account of chaos and confusion and disruption. All that is stable and settled is coming apart. In short, Mark speaks to us of the coming of our Lord.

For who says that Christ and his ministry come in peace and splendor? That is only in our longing and fantasy, not in our experience.

Even if we take the Bethlehem stories that Matthew and Luke tell us, we find that the Christmas pageants have been a bit selective. A stable doesn't smell like pine trees and mothballs, however we remember it from the pageant. Taking the Bethlehem stories literally, what did the occasion mean to the troubled town in the troubled land, a town already beset by political strife, crowded with unwanted and unwilling visitors? According to the stories, it must have meant that uncouth shepherds—for it was to the socially unfit that the shepherding job was assigned—had abandoned their sheep, presumably some of the townsmen's sheep, and were trampling noisily through town in the middle of the night. It meant the arrival of some very suspicious foreigners. And it meant the murder of their infant sons. Can such bleakness and blackness truly be the mood of awaiting and finding Christ? That, in fact, seems to be the Bible's testimony, from Isaiah to Revelation. The path from manger to cross is not so far—only far enough to take up the chaos of our waiting onto the cross. The artist is right to paint the shadow of the cross falling on the infant in the manger.

For it is not easy for Christ to come to us, nor for us to serve him, when our lives are neat and stable. We try so hard to be strong men and undivided and to bind the Lord, his church, and his ministry, in swaddling cloths, and to lay them in a stable place. But our full and ordered house shuts them out—just as the inn at Bethlehem. Perhaps it is just to a divided nation, a ruptured community, a torn family, a split self, chaotic sense of vocation, an impossible church, that Christ and his call comes.

To be sure, there is the risk of building new cathedrals, or a new stable, out of the chaos, just as though the chaos itself can provide building blocks. Some these days try. There is the danger of ripping down the manger scene just because ripping seems itself a good. And the new Christmas message becomes, "Burn, baby, burn." Normlessness becomes the new norm, secularism the new faith, chaos the new Christ. But chaos is not Christ; he does come to chaos. Perhaps we can even let go of our celebration of the confusion; and this for many of us may be the last thing to let go.

When we are in the midst of the hectic, disordered confusion of our lives and our ministries, perhaps we are most likely to find Christ's call, direction, and service—if we can let go of those pleasant memories of the neatly swaddled and stabled Christ and let go of our visions of swaddling him again in a new stable place and discover that he *is* here.

PRISONERS
TO
APPEARANCES—
OR FREED?

Behold! human beings living in an underground den, which has a mouth open toward the light and reaching all along the den; here they have been from their childhood, and have their legs and necks chained so that they cannot move, and can only see before them, being prevented by the chains from turning round their heads. Above and behind them a fire is blazing at a distance, and between the fire and the prisoners there is a raised way; and you will see, if you look, a low wall built along the way, like the screen which marionette players have in front of them, over which they show the puppets, . . . men passing along the wall carrying all sorts of vessels, and statues, and figures of animals made of wood and stone and various materials, which appear over the wall. Some of them are talking, others silent. . . . They are strange prisoners. . . . They see only their own shadows, or the shadows of one another, which the fire throws on the opposite wall of the cave. . . . And of the objects which are being carried in like manner they would only see the shadows.

In this famous fable in book VII of the *Republic*, Plato portrays mankind as prisoners in a cave, chained to face the back wall, where they can see nothing but flickering shadows cast by a fire and moving objects behind them. This fable, and the philosophical system it represents, may or may not depict mankind's actual plight. But most decidedly and most dramatically it does represent the *feelings* many of us, presumably including Plato, have about our situation.

We live out our ideals and visions and hopes with the raw material of daily events, saying particular things, not others, to particular people, not others, who make particular responses, not others, within particular institutions and locations, not others. But these daily events are flickering shadows. True, we know, in principle and "ideally," that these particular expressions must have something to do with the more ultimate and ideal. The education we give and receive must have something to do with the gaining of truth. The way we spend our days must have something to do with our vision of a vocation. What we say and do in our homes and in our churches must have something to do with the fostering of love. The shadows on the wall have to come from somewhere. Love, truth, goodness, beauty, faith, responsibility, hope, vocation, freedom, identity, maturity—these and all the other ideals and aspirations by which we live are nothing to us unless they make their appearance in the stuff of our life. But that appearance is so inevitably ambiguous, so flickering, so impure, that we may with Plato long wistfully for more direct access to the good and the true, the Source of life. We mistrust any particular appearances which the ultimates make in our life, and want to apprehend the ultimates themselves. We want to strip away the husks and hold the kernel in our hands, a grand hermeneutical cleansing of our lives and of Life.

It is something like the child's half-conscious, haunting awareness that there is an unflickering, uncomplicated, pure support for him from his parents despite—or is it because of—the disappointments and incompleteness and turbulence which besets each actual encounter with parents. In the midst of spilled milk, hurry and worry, timidity over showing affection, and all the other conditions in and through which parental love must appear, each appearance of this love is welcomed but also mistrusted because wrapped in ambiguities. Or perhaps it is like the parent's longing to be able to express in a pure and unsullied way the affection he does feel. Or perhaps it is like the writer of a book who feels that there are pure truths to be expressed but never finding the right words for such expression.

The mistrust of the particulars and the longing for direct access to the unconditioned produces an elusive, insatiable quest. As soon as we peel back one layer of appearance in order to get at that which appears, we discover instead, inevitably, only another appearance. Our pursuit to capture the ultimate goes in infinite, if vain (and infantile) regression. Even if Plato's prisoner becomes unchained and turns to see what makes the shadows, he discovers that the source of the shadows is itself only image, facsimile, and imitation. And the fire which casts the light is but a poor precursor of the kind of light that awaits outside the cave. It is as though whatever one possesses or apprehends becomes, thereby, tainted with a kind of inverse Midas touch. To know and to have dealing with is to render into particulars, and therefore to compromise the purity. In principle, Plato urges the possibility of the prisoner casting off the chains and gradually mounting to a poignantly direct confrontation with the Source. But in practice, Plato seems to make it clear that any claim or attempt to do so is invariably contaminated. This same wistful elusiveness is echoed in more modern classics in their urging for *absolute* dependence (Schleiermacher), *radical* monotheism (Niebuhr), or *ultimate* concern (Tillich). To know God is infinitely elusive, because to claim to know God is to know lesser than God, and one must acknowledge a God beyond the god he knows and regret the partialness and the ambiguities of his own particular knowledge.

We feel we live in a precarious tension between the ideals and their appearances, between the ultimates and the particulars, between the spirit and its necessary embodiment.

41

We cannot, to be true to ourselves, live without recognizing the claim of the ideals, the sense of self, the vocational goal, the purposes of the church, and of family, absolute dependence, radical obedience, perfect freedom and faith, and all the rest. Yet these are known and experienced by us only in specifics, which contradict the ideals. We know our self only in particular roles and talents and moments, never as a pure self, but these roles constrict and impair self. We exercise our dependence and obedience only in specific loyalties to particular objects, but these specific loyalties violate the faithful obedience we claim. We know freedom and faith only in particular evidence, but our reliance on these signs denies freedom and faith. Church and ministry and family can have only particular forms and activities, but are not realized in them. The specifics are *the only appearances* of the ideals, but they are also *only the appearances.*

Our peril then is a double one. We can fall off either side. (It may be that ministers are among those who feel especially keenly these double claims, or perhaps, to put it more accurately, those who feel these claims keenly, are very likely to become ministers. See the final chapter.) On one side, there is the risk of taking the appearances as the reality, of absolutizing, idolizing, and idealizing them, of placing absolute loyalties and sense of absolute well-being on particular objects and activities. On the other side, one can become so fearful of this first error that he—like Plato and Schleiermacher and Niebuhr and Tillich, and like many of today's secularizers, on the rebound from particularistic and fundamentalistic expressions of Christianity—puts all his weight against the error of absolutizing the particular. He emphasizes about appearances that they are only appearances and therefore are unworthy and unreliable.

To develop leaders to the highest possible state of manhood, Plato would have had them shuck off most of the entanglements which many of us would suppose actually define and develop manhood, the intimacy of family life, or such responsibilities as the handling of money and property. People who did participate in such human activities were thereby contaminated and not to be trusted. Homer's gods were banned for the same reason. The plight of the prisoners in the Cave is an unnecessary and an avoidable condition. The majority in the cave were blinded by the darkness into absolutizing the appearances and defending the shadows as true reality. This is what terrified Plato, and his solution was to go to the other extreme, to recommend casting off this dilemma of human ambiguity as unnecessary captivity and to go in search of the true light.

One can be so aware of the one-sidedness of Plato's solution that he makes the opposite mistake, the one Plato was so intent to avoid. One can be so sensitive to the elusiveness and the escapism involved in turning one's back on the appearances which we are given, in the search for appearance-free purity, that he lives only by and with the appearances, and disdains the puritans' and purists' criticism. This is, in our times, the error committed or risked by the secularists and activists who scorn the irrelevance of the reflective churchmen or academicians and in the normlessness of their own making can then find sanction for any action or appearance.

FREEDOM IN THE CAVE, NOT FROM THE CAVE

We know, then, what it feels like to be Plato's prisoners. Yes, *Plato's* prisoners. For, whether we are captive to the appearances or captivated by a longing for the Source, our bondage may be forged mostly by our conviction of the discrepancy. From this arises our fear of losing one by committing ourselves to the other, and this fear forges the chains binding us to what we most fear losing. The Christian gospel gives us reasons for feeling this discrepancy bridged. Plato's prisoners must look in one direction to find the particular appearances of life and in the opposite direction to locate their Source. The Christian can look in the same direction to see both. For him, the shadows—probably that is not the apt image, even, at least not flickering shadows—are cast as on a screen in a shadow play, by objects and light all before him. The appearances are faithful clues and links to that which appears in them. The Creator has entered fully into and remains vigorously in the raw material of the world with which each of us contends.

With this conviction we are freed. We are not compelled either to abandon or to absolutize the particulars. This is the Christian freedom to invest oneself in whatever particular place and circumstances and commitments and persons and relationships and institutions in which he finds himself, accepting them fully, for what they are but not being deceived with an illusion that they are more than they are. He can celebrate them for the degree to which the Ultimates (demands, assurances, opportunities) do appear in them. He freely knows also that this occasion is not the same as the ultimate. He may be looking forward to and even working toward improving the appearance to make it more perfectly show forth that which appears in it. But he is not, meanwhile, incapacitated by this knowledge. He is enslaved neither by his over-idealization of the appearance nor by its imperfection. He knows that though it is only an appearance, something does appear in it. He is free to engage the appearance, to invest himself in it, with enthusiasm, unreservedly, and he is free to let it go unreservedly.

The scientific community has adapted this understanding of freedom as a fundamental principle. With the support of his community, and with a trust compounded in equal measure of conviction that his theories contain truth and conviction that they contain error, the scientist ideally is free about his theories. He is free to trust them and free to abandon them. He pursues a particular theory with all the vigor and determination he can muster. He announces it with enthusiasm, defines it with precision, defends it with skill in as vigorous controversy as possible. He is committed to his theory. He believes in it. Yet out of this vigorous activity occasioned by his wholehearted commitment to the theory—as he knows all along—eventually comes a better theory, perhaps of his own making, perhaps of another's. Then, if he is free, and not bound to the theory by a self-justifying needfulness, he is free to abandon the theory as unreservedly as he once was committed to it. New discovery would be impeded equally by clinging to the old theory and by fear of advancing the old because one knew he and it would eventually be proved in error.

PLATONIC PRISONERS

The Platonist, the mistruster of any forms, the longer for the pure and transcendent manifestation, has many forms himself. One of these is as a sideline *spectator*, flirting with or fantasying the involvement and participation he is too timid or too anxious actually to engage. He is neutral, a reporter, a commentator, an analyst. The journalist, the novelist, the minister, the psychologist, are among those who deal with the materials of intimacy and involvement without having to commit themselves to it.

If the suspicion or anxiety or mistrust of the particular appearance is more severe, it may have to be expressed more vigorously, in attacks on the deficiencies of the appearances. Then we may have some form of *prophet*. The prophet pounces on the imperfection in any appearance. Every attempt to express the good, the true, the beautiful, the loving, the faithful, in personal life or in institutional forms, falls short and the prophet is particularly aware of this defect and eager to call it to our attention, perhaps to goad us to try again.

Or we may have, especially in intellectual spheres, the *methodological purist*. He makes a career of criticizing all conclusions (his own or others') because the method of investigation is never pure enough, the mastery of all data never complete enough to warrant a trustworthy conclusion—at least one he is willing to trust himself to.

To anticipate the final chapter, it is difficult not to hear echoes, or at least analogies, of the risks a child takes in going out on a limb of emotional commitment, only to have it sawed off. Just when the child feels most confident of having met parental expectations, and is basking in the anticipation of certain parental approval—this is when the still unpredictable parent, harried by his own particular worries, or for whatever reason, fails to return approval or scathes through with new criticism. Just when the notes in the fingering were finally mastered on the piano, then he scolds for dynamics and expression. The only safety seems to lie in joining the parents' side and being the critic: Don't really try or trust again.

There are certain appearances we learn to be especially suspicious of as mere flickering shadows, and certain ultimates we especially crave for direct, uncontaminated access to. One of these is the experience of forgiveness, cleansing, justification, feeling "all right." This is a kind of ultimate experience, overwhelming and complete. But it must be mediated. The cleansing does not come, much as one may long for it, in a single, total, overwhelming immediate experience. It comes through particular people, words, occasions, symbols. One may well distrust and be discontent with any particular form of mediation, sacrament, scriptural assurance, penance, others' assurances, or whatever. Any one of these may seem effective for a moment. But just as soon as one begins to celebrate this new state of assurance and freedom, he remembers or fears that it is precisely at this moment of committing himself, letting the guard down, fully accepting the acceptance, that he is most vulnerable; that is just when denunciation may or has come most ruthlessly and mercilessly. The guard is up then ever stronger, and the search goes on ever more urgently: new sacraments, new confessions, new verbal formulae, new groups to belong to.*

---

* The child wants to say, "Hug me as I am, not as you want me

There is the mistrust of particular occasions for service. "When saw we thee hungry or naked or thirsty or sick or imprisoned?" The particular fallen traveler by the wayside can't be what we are called to for ministry. This seems too surprising, too unannounced, too unarranged, too trivial, or too demanding an occasion. There are not the signs confirming that this *is* the Lord's call. Something more grand, more elaborate—and inevitably more remote and abstract—must be called for. I must hurry past along the road so that I can get to the city and call a committee or organize an association to develop a program to do something about this. I must write a letter to the editor or to my congressman. I must urge that somebody is appointed, with adequate budget and adequate staff, to take care of this situation. I must tell the dean that the school really ought to have a course on this subject. Such activities of this scope must come closer to realizing what is expected of me. To be a Christian minister is too grand a goal and obligation to be entrusted to any appearances so flickering as a single fallen traveler by the wayside.

There is something overwhelmingly total about any particulars, such as a particular relationship with a fallen traveler. If you stop and help him, then you are committed. He is on your shoulders, even if not on your donkey. There is no dodging, no retreating, even if unexpected discomforts turn up. You can always withhold yourself or withdraw from a committee meeting or a program if things get too intense.

There is a mistrust, especially in our psychologically sophisticated times, over accepting oneself in all of his particularities. Even if I stop for the fallen traveler, or do anything else that might seem acceptable, or even worthy, I

---

to be to meet your own dreams. Kiss me with a cold, with my dirty or ugly face." But parents can't really let themselves go either in offering forgiveness in a total relationship of assurance. They are questing, looking for more too. So they are always sabotaging or qualifying the assurance and support they really want to offer and the child so badly longs for.

know too well the particularities of my own reaction to be able to regard it as acceptable or worthy or faithful response to the Lord. My motives are mixed, or at least identifiable. Although I may seem, perhaps, to others, to be performing ministry, *I* know that this behavior is prompted by particular motives within me and—with our mistrustful "therefore" —need to be regarded with suspicion. Yes, in abstract principle we can affirm that ministry can be performed only by particular persons, operating through whatever motives and postures they may have. But this is an ideal which we are somehow unwilling to acknowledge in our own lives. Can any good come out of such limited motives as mine? These are much too shadowy. Ministry, if it is to be valid, must have expression in some form more obviously worthy.

Set against this is the free Christian's understanding of his own motives. He is neither intimidated nor defensive about the fact that he has them. He doesn't confuse his own motives with ideals of unconditional love and self-giving of a kind of which only God is capable. But neither does he see his own motives as so utterly alien to expressions of God's will and ways. He accepts these motives for what they are, no more, and no less. He knows that behavior guided by them may well prove of worthy service. He also knows that behavior guided by them may be quite erroneous and faulty, and he needs to be open constantly to correction. He will not fear the correction so much that he grovels on the sidelines and refuses to venture forth. But he will accept it gladly when it comes and willingly let go of the patterns he was so thoroughly invested in.

INTERLUDE

THE
MINISTER'S
WORK

Having taken stock of the minister's faith and doubt, I now want to confront some dilemmas of his work. In doing this I turn to three subjects: the minister's goals, his preaching, and his administration.

I want to be as specific as possible in each instance; to discern what are the dilemmas and doubts that are part of what ministers do; to question and challenge some of the routine ways by which purposes, goals, and the daily tasks of ministry are related to and separated from each other.

It is by being specific, by being concerned with the daily tasks and jobs of ministry, that I hope to discover the freedom to minister.

GOALS
AND
GOAL-STICKERS

I invite you, the reader, to begin this chapter by taking time to jot down a few responses to three questions:

1. What is the purpose of the church and its ministry?

2. Picture the person you have known or are still hoping to meet whom you would nominate as an ideal Christian; or, to put it another way, picture the kind of person you hope your ministry can help others become. Describe his behavior in one or two specific situations. What does he do, say, think, feel that marks him as a Christian? Be just as concrete as possible in describing specific actions, thoughts, and words. Picture the person in some particular situation and write the script of how he responds.

3. Recall or imagine a day, or an hour, in which you felt most truly a minister, most faithful in responding to your call, most effective in meeting your intentions for ministry. As concretely as possible, what happened? What did you do, say, think, feel? With what words or behavior did others respond, if their response played a part in confirming this as a moment of ministry?

This chapter is about the dilemma of relating your second and third answers to your first answer.

Perhaps you feel no dilemma. This could mean two different things. (1) It could mean that you have been able to specify concrete marks of the Christian and of the ministry which seem to you obvious and absolutely faithful specifications of your general statement of the church's purpose. Your second and third answers illustrate your first unambiguously. To you, this book is not primarily addressed, as you must already have sensed by now. You are referred to other books, plentiful in number these days, which want to shake up what they will call your complacency or your idolatry, your too-comfortable identification of your particular goals and criteria with God's will for you and yours. But read on here, too, if you would be looking for a context in which to fit such prophetic rebukes. (2) Perhaps you feel no dilemma because your second and third answers have been quite as general as your first answer and are in fact restatements rather than specifications of the first. If your second and third answers are no more concrete than such words as "responsible," "caring," "sensitive," "responsive," you must be sensitive to the dilemma this chapter is about. If you have found yourself not describing actual behavior and actual words with which one could define and recognize "responsible," "caring," etc., you must be keenly aware of the risks and presumption in venturing such specification. Yet risky and presumptuous as it is, we do in fact every day make decisions about the directions in which we will guide our behavior and others'. And we must.

This chapter suggests:

1. That your second and third answers almost certainly do bear some direct relationship to your first answer; that the specifications of your ministry's purpose in answers two and three are, in part, faithfully derived from your general statement of the church's purpose; in other words, that the specified behavior can entail legitimate and important manifestations of the purpose.

2. That the specifications are also related to cultural values and personal motivations; that the specified purposes reflect, in part, what is personally satisfying to you and what your culture has taught you to value; that the specified goals are relative and conditioned.

3. That the personal and cultural roots of your second and third answers make them impure specifications of the general purposes, with the risk that adherence to these specific goals may sometimes—*but by no means inevitably and always,* as some reductionistic social analysts would have it—lead you and yours to contradict, rather than to fulfill the general purposes.

The current debate about the purposes of church and the nature of ministry seldom gets beyond a dispute among alternative specifications: institutional allegiance vs. social responsiveness vs. personal wholeness, etc. In this dispute, one answer to questions two or three is offered as a more pure and faithful expression of general purposes and therefore a perspective from which to judge the impurities and faithlessness of other answers to these same questions. This debate is good—except when advocates of one specification pridefully overlook the fact that *their* concrete purposes are also relative and conditioned. Such dialectic is the best process I know of to keep us constantly retuned to the general purposes that transcend all our specifications and to keep us in the struggle for ever more faithful specifications. But this book is less concerned with resolving any particular debates than with analyzing different kinds of responses which we make to the dilemma.

Therefore, this chapter goes on to suggest:

4. That one way of escaping the torment of the dilemma —of having to specify goals, while knowing that all specifications are relative and faulty—is to overlook the conditioned and impure nature of the specification, to treat it as identical with the general purpose that has called a man to ministry, and therefore as deserving of absolute loyalty. This is a sell-out; such a one is stuck on the goals he has listed in answers two and three, unable to experience the correction of answer one.

5. That another way of avoiding the torment—and one more characteristic of many of us—is to become so aware of the tainted impurity of all specifications, that one therefore avoids all specifications; ministry remains abstracted from life and always on the verge; this is a cop-out, in the name of an unachievable purity; such a one is stuck on the goals he has listed in answer one and unable to move to two or three.

6. That the Christian message to the first group is the hope for freedom, a freedom to let go, when necessary, of the particular goals and criteria to which they are so explicitly committed or even addicted. This is the hope for a freedom to relinquish their absolute loyalty to the relative specifications.

7. That the Christian message to the second group is the hope for freedom, a freedom to let go and run the risk of idolatry; a freedom to relinquish their absolute concern with purity; a freedom to recognize the degree to which particular, even institutionalized, objectives *do* embody that which transcends them.

A SUNDAY DIARY

Here are some signals given off by one church as to how it specifies its objectives. All of these experiences actually occurred to me on a single Sunday. Each of them expresses some specific expectations on behalf of the church, or one church, or some church members. At the start of the day, I ask myself the question, "What does the church want me to be or do in order to be a more faithful member, or more a Christian?" Here are some of the answers:

A deacon greeted me in the narthex, "Good morning, brother—I guess I can still call you brother, since you haven't grown a beard yet."

As I sat in a pew, the woman in front of me admonished her girl, "No more whining, now. We are in church."

There was considerable head-turning and whispering among the pews, apparently expressing disapproval, and apparently focused on a young man who had come in wearing a large bulky sweater, no tie, and jeans.

During the service, the minister mentioned two events, one that evening and one Wednesday, and he made it clear that he thought that Christian commitment implied an obligation to be present at each of these events.

In the narthex after the service, one person said to me, "I am glad that some of us stayed home to be religious today, instead of going off to look at the leaves."

Someone else engaged me in discussion on a local election issue, ending with the resounding affirmation, "We aren't Christian if we don't stand up and make clear what we think on these issues!"

During the afternoon I was asked if I would do my duty by canvassing to raise money for the church this fall.

When I went to the church meeting that evening, I heard among other things, a long speech against sex education in the public schools in which it was said that church people must take a stand against indecent movies and premarital sex.

These were all helpfully concrete and specific recommendations as to how one behaves if he is to be a faithful Christian and church member (and, of course, these particular recommendations make no distinction between being Christian and being a church member). These are seen as criteria of the Christian life, and the purpose of the church is to make people more Christian by faithful obedience to these criteria.

But I also heard that morning another statement of criteria and purposes. This was far more general and abstract. The sermon spoke of "making real the love of God among us." It was quite apparent that every one of my other informants, those who had flashed to me the other signals of criteria and purposes, wholly endorsed this general principle. They would each want to say that the mark and task of Christian and of church is "to make real the love of God among us."

So I am left with evidence of these concrete expectations as marks of the Christian: no beard, no whining, conventional dress, attendance at Sunday morning worship and at other church-sponsored events, financial support of the church, vigorous expression of political opinion, support of particular codes concerning films and sexual behavior. And I have the general statement of the mark of the Christian, to make real the love of God among men. The same people proposed to me the general and the concrete criteria. What is the relationship between such specific and concrete criteria and such general and lofty goals?

The concrete as expressions of the general. One cannot dismiss too easily the concrete criteria I encountered on this particular Sunday as though they had nothing to do with the general statement of purpose I also encountered. Certain conventions of appearance, behavior, and dress, support for the institutional church, ultimate concern-like expression of political convictions—such things have been deeply embedded through a lifetime in the religious orientation of these persons and an intimate component of their relationship to God. There is a genuine sense in which it can be said that they may know no other way to "make real the love of God among us" than just in such behavior as I found them recommending. To take away concrete criteria might be to wrench from them the principal means by which they have been able to apprehend and to respond to the love of God.

But such concrete criteria can have a logical as well as a psychological relationship with the more general statement. Most of my Sunday morning goal-setters would have been quite capable of developing a rational and persuasive account of the connection between the goal they advanced and the rhetoric of the sermon which they endorsed. Disruptive noise and appearance in the worship service becomes an impediment to others, and hence a contradiction of God's love; what I am free to do myself I am not free to do if I offend my brother. Sexuality has always been recognized as a special gift of God, such intimate human love bearing a relationship to transcendent divine love, and profaning the former risks profaning the latter. A political issue, in becoming the occasion for expressing one's ultimate concern, can become a religious occasion, involving a profound sense of caring responsibly and manifestly for others.

Concrete criteria as expressions of the culture and contradictions of Christian purpose. If the above arguments are more commonly made by church members, the other half of the case is far more commonly made these days by those who write about church members. It could undoubtedly be demonstrated that every one of the criteria advanced by my Sunday morning informants derives from their involvement in a limited suburban subculture and from personal motivations. The support of established institutions like the church, the good citizen role in politics, conventional appearance and dress, ascetic self-denial, whether of colorful leaves or colorful movies—such things are marks of membership in established suburban communities, not of membership among God's people. They serve more to quell personal anxieties than to promote the love of God.

And again, the case can be made not only by psychological analysis, but also by logical argument. To demonstrate history and functions is not automatically to demonstrate contradiction of Christian principles, the argument *can* proceed to the second point: that arbitrary restrictions on dress and behavior, narrow institutional loyalties, heedless dogmatism whether political, religious, or moral—all of these constrictions manifestly impede the recognition and celebration of "the love of God among men."

DIARY OF A MINISTRY AND HISTORY OF A CHURCH

If a single church member has difficulty reconciling the general declarations about the nature of the Christian life which he hears on a given Sunday morning with the concrete clues which he also hears on the same Sunday as to what identifies and marks a Christian—if a single church member has difficulty in making this reconciliation, and if a single church has difficulty in faithful specification of its purposes, then they are squarely in the middle of the history of the Christian church. It is in the nature of the faith that it demands immanent expression in forms and institutions, concrete criteria, particular purposes. It is also in the nature of the faith that it transcends, both judging and fulfilling, any such lodging. Faithful specification is demanded. Faithful specification is impossible. The Christian worships a God who became incarnate—and the Son of man had no place to lay his head, and was crucified.

A Christian, a minister, a church, the church is gripped by a vision, by a call. This can be verbalized in general and abstract formulae—liturgical, theological, and rhetorical formulae—especially at such times as baptism, ordination, installations, annual meetings, and church councils. But churches do not live by ordination rhetoric and synod proclamation alone, though they cannot live without it. And a ministry is not formed—a minister's daily decisions about priorities and purposes and programs are not guided —by formulae alone, though this cannot be done without them. How will a minister, or a generation of ministers, specify purposes and set priorities? What are the marks of ministry in their time by which they can guide and judge their efforts? How do they want their people to be different, as a result of their ministry? Ministers—whether Paul, Jonathan Edwards, or you—who venture to struggle with this question sentence themselves to perpetual torment—since their transcendent vision both compels them to specification of purpose and also judges as inadequate every such specification. And it is only the freedom and trust that comes from finding themselves grounded in the transcendent vision and not in the specification that permits them to withstand this torment.

The minister has plenty of models, no less prestigious than Barth, Kierkegaard, or Plato, for avoiding the torment by supposing that the transcendent, in principle, eludes—not just judges—any specification. Or he can avoid the torment by following those models who find the specification easy, obvious, and unchallengeable: What is the clear, unambiguous index of Christian faith? Some Pentecostals would say glossolalia, some fundamentalists would say profession of the inerrancy of scripture, some ministers would say regular attendance at church, some moralists would say conformity with a limited set of behavioral prescriptions. But the risk is that with the torment avoided, so is the faith which requires and sustains and judges efforts at the faithful specification of the transcendent.

Typical specifications. What are the specifications of purpose commonly held by or urged upon ministers today? I cite below some typical answers to questions two and three.

Every one of these specifications can be interpreted as a borrowing from or an appeal to values and goals that are abroad and prestigious in the secular culture. Every specification is therefore relative, conditioned, culture-bound, accommodative. Inevitably, therefore, each specification must finally become an affront to the faithful vision it would specify. Wholehearted commitment to any one of the specifications, therefore, inevitably becomes an idolatry.

Allegiance to each can, therefore, be interpreted as expressing loyalty to the secular which suggests and sanctions the specifications, as readily as loyalty to the faith which is being specified. Every specification is eventually rebuked, in the name of purity, for being a sell-out, a skimpy and hasty baptism of secular values to enhance the rosters of the apparent faithful, a yielding of principle to gain power, the pathetic preference for being relevant rather than being faithful. Thus one generation can accuse preceding generations of having abandoned the faith by accommodating to the architecture, ritual, and political system of pagan Rome, to medieval superstition and pageantry, to political authorities or to political rebels, to an unduly high enjoyment of marriage and family (whether by Luther or American suburbanites), to frontier individualism, to fear-erected monolithic social bastions (whether of communistic or American establishment), etc. Thus one faction invariably accuses another faction of subverting the faith by identifying it with highly limited and passing cultural values, whether regional folk morality, psychological therapeutics, hippie fadism, antiscientific know-nothingism, political liberalism, suburbanism, black racism, white racism, whether a kind of neo-Marxist preoccupation with economic forces, or psychological yearnings for stability and status quo, or psychological yearnings to be personally effective in producing social change, etc., etc.

The accusation that one's specification of the Christian faith is a reflection of and accommodation to cultural values is the familiar and necessary stock-in-trade of reformers. They are joined these days by sociological analysts—critics who seem rather startled to discover that they can discern, even measure the cultural elements of American religious movements, and who frequently proceed to two non sequiturs: (1) this situation is new (they confuse their fresh discovery with the advent of what they have discovered), and

(2) the transcendent is denied. What understandably eludes both reformers and sociological critics is the recognition that the cultural accommodation is inevitable and intended and that it is as faithful as one can be. The Christian finds God and faith in incarnate and historical forms and announces God and faith in incarnate and historical forms. The Christian church and the Christian minister does not progress from accommodation to purity, but from accommodation to accommodation.

Here are some characteristic responses to the second question posed at the outset of this chapter.

Knowing well. "Knows what he believes and why. . . . Well prepared and attends the Sunday evening study group. . . . Somebody I know I am reaching with my sermons. . . . Answers me back on my sermons." "I am a teacher in all I do. Children and adults must be taught the faith. That's why it's given to us in a book."

Conceptualization and articulation of the faith and its implications is an undeniable component of the call to be Christian and the call to be minister, and arguments can be mustered aplenty to contend that it is a crucial component. But the minister who gives it such priority almost certainly does so for other reasons as well: he is well trained at the conceptual tasks. His principal models throughout his training have been those who excelled at conceptualization and articulation above all else; they have set standards at this task and rewarded him when he met them. He is perhaps more proficient at and more accustomed to this skill than anything else, and perhaps some very happy and warm memories are associated with keenly intellectual discussions in seminary and conferences. For such a minister, it is understandable why he should emphasize this element of the Christian's and the minister's task, and there is no reason to suppose that it is not absolutely appropriate and absolutely faithful to his call to regard this section of the vineyard as his assignment.

Except, such an emphasis—because it means so much personally—may become so strong that ministry is constricted, that the minister may sometimes impose this specific goal where it is inappropriate and may be deaf to other calls to ministry. Attention is restricted to those who most nearly possess the skills to reproduce a theological seminar for the minister, perhaps to the point of selecting an elite congregation, as of college students, for whom one will work. People are scolded or enticed to become serious students, but in the process of scolding and enticing the minister may unwittingly deny even the very elements of faith he wants to affirm. He may be so concerned to lift them to his criteria of a Christian life that his scolding and his enticing assumes an irrational, manipulative form, denying the very element of rational conceptualization he wants to affirm. His scolding and enticing may prevent his communicating of other elements of the faith such as a gracious unconditional regard for a personality.

When the woman says, "I wish we said grace more at home," he may engage her in discussion of prayer or on the secularization of American culture. But if her remark is in fact a plea for ministry to rising guilt feelings or to a gradually disintegrating family, or for help in sharing the bounty of her home, then *this* ministry will be neglected.

Aware of this difficulty, a minister might forthrightly declare to himself, on leaving seminary, that he would abandon, perhaps even sacrifice, such conceptual pursuits at which he has become so adept and on which he has become so dependent, for the sake of being responsive to the actual needs of his people. But such a renunciation is no less a mutilation of ministry.

Is it possible that a man could enter into his ministry both with the freedom to throw himself and his people fully into conceptual tasks, but also the freedom to withdraw and acknowledge that these are limited and partial approximations of the Christian life? Could he lead the woman in an intense discussion of the role of prayer in the midst of contemporary secularization—then lean back and confess, "But maybe that is only what I am interested in and not at all what concerns you." He has taken her question seriously, and taken it seriously with the most serious part of himself, where he really is. And perhaps it has reached her. But having done his thing, and done it as wholeheartedly as he can, in now admitting that it was only his thing, he invites her to do hers. The invitation may be more readily accepted both because he has not hesitated fully and seriously to put himself and his perspective on the table and also because he has been equally free to take himself and his perspective off of the table.

Doing good. One theological student answered a question like number three by describing an experience during his summer work in a rural poverty area. He had befriended and had been cordially received by a large impoverished family. The man was unemployed "and so spent most of his time on the front porch drinking beer." The children were without shoes and largely illiterate. "Once I suppose," the student reported, "I would have figured I needed to get them into church, or at least do some Bible-reading with them, but I don't have those hang-ups any more. Now I know that that would be just what I said—what *I needed*—and not necessarily what they needed or what God called me to do for them."

He set out to meet their needs and after some effort, he arranged two job interviews for the man, raised enough money for shoes for all of the children, and brought books along to spend time with the children. "Now I felt I was doing what Jesus was really talking about."

Indeed, he was. The student had every reason to suppose that this kind of service to human needs was required and warranted by scripture, by the best of traditions of the church, by the most prominent of contemporary church proclamations, by the highest of religious instincts.

But, alas, there is more to the story. The man failed to

show up for either job interview, and when the student sought him out, was still on the front porch in his undershirt drinking beer. On his next visit after delivering the money for the shoes, the student noticed the children were still barefoot and asked about the money. "They hadn't had any ice cream for such a long time, I thought they deserved a little party," the mother explained. And the children did not sit still for a very long reading lesson. Is it possible that the student was still missing ministry to their needs by pursuing steadfastly his own goals? Regular employment, proper dress, the skills of reading—these were such high values in the subculture in which the student was raised, and they were so firmly instilled in him, that he assumed without thinking that these *were* and *should be* universally acknowledged as supreme goals and signs of life.

But the reply obviously indicates that they were not so recognized, and raises some question about the "should be." Is it possible that the student was "hung up" on work, shoes, and reading quite as much as he once was "hung up" on attending church and reading the Bible, and for much the same reasons? He was trained to regard these as supreme marks of the good and full life, and he was determined to perform, indeed, to "achieve" what could be recognized as effective ministry. Yet in the determination to achieve marks of ministry for himself and marks of the fulfilled life for the family, could he have been overlooking and impeding ministry and the full life? Was a determined commitment to these particular goals worsening rather than improving still more fundamental needs of the family, such as for respect and sense of integrity, and for an "unconditional sense of acceptance"?

Employment, clothing, and an education—and a personal sense of "doing good"—are appropriate and authentic specifications of ministry—on some occasions—but also so culturally and psychologically conditioned that they are quite clearly relative, not absolute, and, on other occasions, inevitable impediments to ministry.

What this one case highlights, of course, is a persistent dilemma, especially of American Protestantism, which has often incorrectly identified individual achievement, especially economic and educational achievement, with the Christian life. The Calvinistic *doctrine* may be suitably cautious, regarding such achievements only as a *sign*, with only a *probable* reliability of salvation. But the Calvinism in men is intolerant of probability and searches for sure signs, to the point of identifying the signs and what they signify.

What are different ways of responding to such frustrated efforts at ministry as the student experienced? The student might have remained determinedly committed/addicted to doing these goods. He might have done this by badgering or manipulating the family into accepting the goods he wanted to deliver. He might have done this by abandoning the family in his frustration; if they could not accept these goods, they could not be ministered to. In the former case he could quote Paul on perseverance, and in the latter case quote Jesus on shaking the dust off his feet, and in each case indicate by quoting scripture how he identified his objectives as unmistakable fulfillment of the commission Paul had accepted and Jesus rendered.

In fact, in reflecting on his summer experience, the student responded in quite the other extreme, in a direction more characteristic, I think, of readers of this book, though in extreme form. He felt chagrined and guilty at recognizing that he had been trying to achieve a particular kind of satisfaction from "doing good," by imposing his own limited values on someone else, to whom they did not belong. He experienced their rejection of his goods as a divine judgment and as a conversion experience. He took the position that these values "are only the suburban values my parents drilled into me." And he renounced such "conventional values" as unsuitable not only to impose on the rural family but also unsuitable for himself to follow. If the values of achievement and propriety were culturally induced, then they were tainted. He began acting out his repudiation of these values, in the "hippie" fashion of his time, in a self-proclaimed search for pure and untainted values, "where God is really at and what he really wants me to do." This initially appeared to take the form of adopting the life-style of the rural family, as though they, untainted by suburban middle-class culture, were somehow thereby culture-free, and therefore "closer to God." His quest was, of course, doomed to a discovery that the barefoot-beer-undershirt-front porch game was no less a game and no less a cultural cul-de-sac than the church-going, Bible-reading game, or the hard work, clean clothes, clean-living game. It was just as relative, just as culturally conditioned, just as great an impediment to the discovery of God's grace and God's direction as the other—though it was also no less an authentic possibility for the vehicle or the arena in which grace and direction might be discovered.

What would it mean for the student to have responded "in freedom"—not completely selling out to values of achievement and propriety as though these were recommended by God to all people for all times and not just recommended by his parents and their suburban culture—and not copping out as though work could never serve as a gracious gift or as a call to responsibility, as a sign of participating in a Christian life under God. What if the student were clearly open to the possibility of presenting work as an offering and as an expectation which the man drinking beer on the porch could be expected to take with a kind of ultimate seriousness? And what if he were opened with equal freedom to the possibility that the work is only his own offering and expectation, and not God's? How might he exercise such a ministry in freedom? Could the student admit that he is caught, that he is committed to a goal which is, to say the least, not shared by the object of his concern, "I guess I set up these appointments without asking you much about it." If the student can level a bit, perhaps the man can too, "I'm not so sure that's the right job for me." So the conversation is begun which, in effect, could be understood as a combined search by two people for direction, for a more faithful and more authentic specification of God's intentions, his vocation for them both. If the man's misgivings turn out to center around his own sense of inadequacy to enter into a different life-style, the student's very act of consulting and leveling turns out to be a mark of assurance and supportive caring that ministers directly to his needs. If the man's reluctance turns out to be based on the anger and anxiety generated by past occasions on which he has made an effort to work only to be rejected or cheated, again the student's stance of inquiring and caring opens the way of ministry as neither insisting upon nor abandoning the goal of work ever could. If the student shows himself different from the pushers (social workers?) and cheaters (employers?), then maybe they can work together to confront the others. The ministry has been occasioned by the freedom to push the job as a serious goal, combined with the freedom to stand back and view the pushing objectively in a larger context. Important issues for the man's life could be brought to focus and to discussion by the pushing of the job. The discussion could proceed freely and truthfully if the pushing of the job was seen as being the starting point for the discussion, and not as predetermining its outcome.

Doing well. The minister can hardly define his ministry for anyone without warranting the question: Am I trying to make them more like me, or more like what they are intended to be? For it is likely to be his firm presupposition that life is measured by doing good, doing well, or just doing. And those who are deprived of doing are deprived of life. The ministry to retired people is specified as keeping them busy. Help for the retarded is offered in the form of teaching them to do productive things. As the expression has it, the degree to which anyone is "active in the church" is a generally accepted mark of his Christian commitment.

In casting about for ways to assist ghetto residents, one

minister became incensed at the high charges black people were assessed for funerals and he set out to shield such "victims of exploitation." Here is the pragmatic criterion of productive utility in another form. Money spent on display is money taken from such "practical" needs as food, clothing, and shelter. One must spend his money as well as his time productively.

Obviously the concern for a person's productivity and accomplishment, for effectively addressing the practical problems of his life and his times—obviously such concern can hardly be separated from a religious ministry to him. But equally obviously, we are on the brink of sabotaging a Christian ministry to the degree that we find ourselves suggesting that such accomplishment is a necessary condition for wholeness or acceptability or the fulfilled life. There are many other values clustered under such rubrics as "celebration," or just "being." The prodigal and heedless gifts of God hardly invite, as appropriate response, effort, and calculated budgeting of getting and spending. Others' styles of being, enjoying, celebrating may be fully as much a corrective of the minister's limited criteria of doing as much as it is an occasion for his pity and "ministry."

Faced with such a dilemma, a minister may persist in pressing the specific goals he holds most dear. He may abandon the pressing of any specific goals because their cultural boundedness risks blundering. That is, he may try to serve the transcendent either by pushing his values or by yielding his values. Or he may find a freedom in ministering, willing both to push his values and to yield his values, in search for and testimony to transcendent values.

When the minister concerned about funeral costs discovered that his educational and organizational ministries were falling short of enthusiastic response from the "victims" he would save, he took a second look. He neither persisted steadfastly nor abandoned his task. Instead he raised the question with black leaders as to where there was good and where there was misdirection in his efforts. In effect, to what degree were his goals pointing toward more transcendent goals, and to what degree were they pointing toward more personal and limited values which deflected his efforts from the transcending goals? Although the answer was murky at first, it finally came clear and perfectly understandable: efforts at the welfare of the people were welcome, and indeed the goal of spending money to meet serious human needs could not be discounted. But ostentatious funeral display, undesirable from one point of view, had to be recognized as serving important functions. Under conditions of oppression and denial of selfhood, funerals provided one self-restoring affirmation; let the psychologist call it a "compensation" if he wishes. The funeral displays were less a wrong than a symptom of wrongs. Reduce the oppression and denial of selfhood, and one will reduce the need for "impractical" funeral display. Helped thus—as a consequence of the confrontation—to see his goals in larger perspective, the minister resumed his efforts on the larger front.

Being good. "He has worked hard all his life—at his job, or for the scouts or for the church or keeping his house up. He sent all his children to college, though I think he never earned more than $35 a week. Always firm with his children; he knew exactly what he expected and why. But he was just as firm with himself, one glass of wine every Saturday night and that was all. No smoking; in fact, except for that glass of wine, he probably never spent a penny on personal pleasure for himself. A living embodiment of the ten commandments and the Golden Rule. Never even got a parking ticket. Never any question about his devotion to his family. No one ever heard him raise his voice in anger to another person. Always doing things for other people."

Such a portrait of the Christian hero is as likely as any to be the model held before most American Protestant ministers as they were growing up. None would want seriously to dispute it as *an* authentic expression of Christian life. Yet it is highly significant that such a portrait corresponds only slightly, if at all, to the portrait of the ideal Christian that would be drawn by Christians of other centuries and other places. And it is no accident that such an ideal thrives best in small towns of the middle and southern United States. The ideal meets well the requirements of such small town culture, and its development and popularity can probably be attributed as much to the functions it serves for such a culture as it can to the Bible and Christian tradition. In short, this specification of the Christian life is as relative to particular times and places as is any specification. It is as equally vulnerable to becoming absolutized as is any specification, to being proclaimed as the concrete account of the Christian life which must be the ideal for all times and places.

When a Christian minister, or perhaps more commonly a Christian theological student, discovers that these specifications of the Christian life are relative and not absolutely generalizable—when he discovers, as he is likely to say, that "values are changing"—he may react in extreme form. Suddenly discovering that the set of values once offered him as absolute requirements by God are not absolute requirements (or if they are, only by his small town) he may disdain these and all values. He may resolve "never to get in that value box again." If these prescriptions of personal conduct turn out to be the voice of the community as much as the voice of God, then he might as well disregard all prescriptions. He would find God, as it were, by disdaining the voice of the community which he hears in these prescriptions.

But this is to cop out of the struggle to discern authentic values, a struggle which is a mark of life and of the Christian life and a fruit and mark of Christian freedom—as much as "freedom" may be used to rationalize the cop-out.

Being well. "In pastoral counseling, I feel I am doing my

best work, touching people's lives where it is important, and even healing."

"I want people to get rid of their hang-ups, so they can be Christian."

"She keeps her cool in tight committee meetings, doesn't get upset when others do."

"Koinonia groups—where we can let our hair down and be ourselves and be accepted as ourselves."

"He knows how to *listen* to other people."

Healing, koinonia, attending to others, spreading peace and goodwill, removing beams from one's own eyes, and removing other psychological barriers to faith and life— of course these are things that scripture, tradition, and our own religious intuition tell us to aim for. These are common and appropriate objectives of churches, ministers, and members. If such objectives sound like those of psychotherapy, T-groups, sensitivity training, and if ministers and members sometimes feel as though they are in psychotherapy or T-groups, then thank God that he has brought psychotherapy and T-groups into being and used them to remind the church of its purpose. There *is* an authentic relation between these answers to questions two and three and most answers to number one.

Yet it may also be true that clergy adopt such goals more because the current culture says they are good than because the Bible says so. Mental health, adjustment, psychological freedom—prime values in our culture, these days. When the clergyman and church are fostering these values, clergyman and church are sanctioned by the culture as useful and welcome citizens; clergyman and church feel effective and relevant—and faithful. And it would be pious illusion to suppose that their discovery of and commitment to these goals was not largely a consequence of this satisfaction and this endorsement.

Which view is correct? Do the statements of purpose quoted above reflect Christian purposes? Or do they reflect personal satisfactions and yearnings and cultural accommodation?

It is precisely *not* the purpose of this chapter to argue between these two views. It is precisely the point of the chapter that the attempt to choose between these views is futile and faulty. To recognize that his objectives have both transcendent orientation and human motivation should make the Christian no more surprised or uncomfortable than his understanding of Christ as God and man. The "genetic fallacy," the stubborn illogical sense that identification of psychological and cultural roots must be reductionistic and invalidate ideas pointing beyond these roots, has been exposed and denounced by every psychologist of religion, from James and Freud on.

Yet this sense does persist and causes alarm. Regardless of the theology or the logic of the case, we do feel uncomfortable with the recognition that our specific goals may be culturally conditioned. We experience such recognition as accusation that they are impure. When we, or another, discover that our purposes are serving psychological and cultural functions, we gratuitously and apologetically add an "only" and say they are *only* serving psychological and cultural functions.

So, intolerant of the relative and the ambiguous, we pursue our hunt to capture the absolute—either by absolutizing the relative (psychological health and candid group interaction is the hallmark of the Christian life; other goals must be subordinated; statements of purpose which challenge these must be attacked or accommodated), or by repudiating the relative in courageous, quixotic affirmation of the transcendent (pastoral counseling is only a passing fad, a way that the insecure minister makes himself feel good; the true minister must not get caught in such fads, and must serve God!). But either reaction is equally idolatrous and disloyal to the transcendent, the one for identifying it with one cultural value, the other for supposing that it can be captured by the verbal affirmation. In both cases, the transcendent is deprived of its transcendence, and of its capacity to judge and fulfill.

This discomfort with the actual materials of life is what this book is about. To this plight, the book does not want to minimize the struggle and stress and chance for failure and faithlessness which is involved in trying to find concrete expressions for transcendent purposes. It only wants to affirm that entering this struggle—far from abandoning God and his ministry—is to join God and to enter his ministry.

CONSTRUCTING A CHAPTER AS RISKY INVESTMENT

Preaching is only one of many possible roles or activities that could be used as an illustration in the next chapter. To base the chapter on the illustration of preaching itself requires an uneasy commitment and investment by the author. To make this investment I go through the same agony as I suggest in the chapter the minister does in his deciding to preach. To put all of one's communicative eggs in one basket is a risky thing to do. Preaching is too conventional an activity to be interesting to some readers. For others, it is too crucial to be open to analysis. It doesn't lend itself to making some of the points I want to make in this chapter. Yet, to talk about ministry, one must talk about some particular expression of ministry—just as to express ministry he must do it in particular forms with particular people in particular places and institutions.

So, to express my ideas about ministry, I must talk about preaching, or something equally particular. But to talk about preaching, or anything equally particular is to constrict and impair my ideas about ministry.

An author's alternatives to this unwelcome, necessary constriction/expression of his ideas are popular but unsatisfactory. I can avoid the constriction and distorting limitations by trying to talk about "ministry" more generally. But this inhibition over investing the ideas into particular illustrations sacrifices the expression. Ministry cannot be most meaningfully discussed—just as it cannot be most meaningfully practiced—except in terms of particular forms and activities. On the other hand, an author can avoid the dilemma by riding hard the expression in this particular illustration and ignoring the constriction and limitation. I can talk so energetically and thoroughly about preaching as to lose sight of the limited use it can serve my purposes at this point. But to lose sight of the limitations is often to lose sight of the broader purposes. And the author—like preachers who follow this same horn of the dilemma—may find themselves devoting themselves exclusively to preaching for its own sake rather than as an expression of the purposes which led him to it.

I can only hope that my use of this illustration, in its own trivial way, is done in the same spirit of freedom and investment that I covet for ministers as the mood for their ministry. I hope that I will not be inhibited by the prospective limitations from investing my energies and attention thoroughly into the illustration and exploiting it for every grain of its value to us. I hope that I won't fear going out on a limb. But I also hope that I will not become so thoroughly ego-invested in the illustration that I cannot freely abandon it when that too is needful for my intended purposes. I am willing to abandon the limb or even have it broken off—as all limbs must eventually do—when it no longer supports me.

One final remark about the freedom to invest myself and my purposes in the limited illustration of preaching—and indeed in the still more limited illustration I am presently immersed in, of my choice of preaching as an illustration. The free investment in the illustration, as in any going out on a limb, is greatest (and is perhaps made possible at all) when it comes not "in spite of" an awareness of limits, but when it comes *because of* these limits. Here is the freeing confidence that in the reaching of limits—in the breaking of limbs—is the best occasion for still more fruitful expression. Creative-redemptive processes are most readily and most pointedly mobilized at points of limitation and rupture. If some reader is provoked by this chapter into throwing it aside and thinking his own better thoughts, then that will be—I pray I have the freedom to say this honestly—the most welcome use of the chapter. I think it is more likely to happen fruitfully the more concretely I try to express myself.

PREACHING
AS
RISKY
INVESTMENT

Preaching is one of the functions of the minister with compelling warrants in tradition and in experience, perhaps the function with the clearest warrants of all. To be a minister is, among other things, or above all else, to be a preacher. In some minds, preaching is all there is to ministry. Yet preaching has gross deficiencies as an expression of ministry, and to invest oneself and one's ministry earnestly into the activity of preaching is so to constrict ministry (and self) as to distort it.

Some ministers may be so thoroughly and uncritically invested in the preaching role that they identify ministry with preaching, and thereby sacrifice ministry. Some ministers may be so critically aware of the defects and limits of preaching that they stand aloof from the pulpit, and thereby sacrifice ministry. Most ministers probably vacillate in the ambivalence, going through the motions of preaching, but half-heartedly, or with low depression—and thereby sacrifice ministry—because they know full well that their preaching cannot do what it ought to. We can celebrate and envy those ministers who can freely throw themselves into a sermon, just as though it *were* the full and perfect word of God, and just as freely stand back, with humor and contrition, and recognize how far short of communicating the Word of God the sermon has fallen, and how much more ministry is still needed—for in the free, total investment of self in sermon, and in the free, total separation of self from sermon, there lie the greatest opportunities for ministry.

The same can be said of any other function of the ministry, or any other institutional form of the church and its mission—and will be said before this chapter is finished. Ministry and church do not exist apart from expression in particular activities and forms, yet expression in any particular activities and forms is to constrict and distort that which they would express. I bring up this dilemma not to prove it exists—that has already been amply done in the literature of our times. Nor do I intend to point the path to a happy resolution of the dilemma. I bring it up rather to recognize the haunting predicament it poses for the minister and to examine some of the characteristic responses he makes to it.

HOW PREACHING IMPEDES MINISTRY

Here are some of the limitations a minister may recognize as he considers investing a significant amount of his energies, time, and relationship with his people—that is, a significant amount of himself—into the activity of preaching. For one thing, it *is* traditional, and its patterns are traditional, and it may be excrutiatingly difficult for both preacher and hearers to break out of sleepy patterns and to discover ways of communication that grip real issues for real people in our time. Something about the pulpit, perhaps its very heritage and importance, seems to stifle crispness, vitality, engagement, and spontaneity which may emerge readily in other contexts, for example in a discussion group. Further, preaching is only one limited form of ministry and to choose to maximize it is, intentionally or not, to choose to minimize other forms of ministry. This is true first, of course, because time is limited; really to invest oneself into preaching is to commit large amounts of time and energy to this task, which are necessarily not available for other tasks. But preaching may monopolize something even more important than time. It may come to control a minister's relationship with his people. The very act of preaching puts a distance, severity, and uni-directionality in the relationship between the preacher and the preached-to, which inevitably impairs other possible relationships. To be sure, some styles of preaching may mitigate this problem and some aspects of a minister's self may be revealed and known through his preaching in a way that enhances other relationships. But a minister investing his self in preaching knows that in doing so he is precluding and cutting off other important relationships with some people. How can people "level," in business meeting or counseling or picket line, with the man who has so convincingly occupied the lofty height of the pulpit.

A prospective investor in preaching must also face two facts candidly and give pause before their combined recognition: one is the rich psychological satisfactions he may derive from preaching, and the other is the scarcity of evidence that his preaching is having the objective effects among his people that he would wish. That walk from chancel to narthex, after the sermon, can be a disheartening moment, imposing a change in mood as abrupt and as icy as a sunbather's dunking in a cold lake. For in the narthex at noon, he must stoke the burning involvement and whatever sense of triumph he may feel in the morning's sermon and prepare for the casual nonchalance or the tangential enthusiasms or the gushy sentiment with which his sermon is most often greeted. This weekly reaction must raise nearly disastrous doubts about the validity of his investment in the preaching.

The prospective investor in preaching also will consider the particular limitations his own preaching will have. The preaching will demand more than he can offer: insight into the faith, and personal commitment to it, empathy with his people, facility at communication. He must further acknowledge the unreadiness of his own people to hear the word preached in the images of the Bible and the vocabulary of faith, with which he knows how to communicate.

These are some of the defects of preaching. Are these reasons for not preaching or at least not investing oneself in preaching, for going through the motions but without hope or commitment or vision? The same limitations apply —the partialness, the ineffectiveness, the unreadiness, the tainted self-satisfying motivations, the impediments of tradition (or the over-enthusiasms of faddishness)—in whatever direction, whether traditional or experimental, a minister may turn to find expression of his ministry—teaching, counseling, direct social action, discussion groups, administration, political involvement—and under whatever guiding image—enabler, pastoral director, shepherd, crisis repairman, or whatever.

What is a minister to do in the face of such ambiguity? Does he immerse himself heedlessly and so fervently into his preaching (or other form) that he can overlook these limitations? Or does he preserve his integrity and testify to his loyalty to the values that transcend the forms by withholding himself from a vigorous commitment to the preaching role? Is he most concerned to protect himself from irrelevance or irresponsibility by getting fully and actively involved, in preaching or some other role? Or is he most concerned to protect himself from idolatry by a cool, half-hearted participation in preaching (or other forms) so as to testify that he doesn't "believe in" these forms, but only in what transcends them?

Perhaps this dilemma is most debated these days as it applies to "experimental" forms of ministry and to direct social action. Here unqualified enthusiasm and total commitment of "activists" draws either praise or reproof, according to which horn of the dilemma one judges from. From the purist's vantage point, most sensitive to the transcendent criteria and to the partialness and inadequacy of any expression (experimental or traditional), such total investment of oneself may seem unwarranted and idolatrous. The activist disparages just such aloofness because it presupposes a spurious never-to-be-attained perfection, and he insists the transcendent values find reality only as they find full incarnation in living (not half-living) persons.

But, whether for an activist, experimental, or traditional form, must one choose one horn of the dilemma or the other? Or is there a way of participating, fully not half-heartedly, yet responsibly not recklessly? Can one "believe in" preaching—accept it as a fully valid and worthy form —yet not "believe in" preaching—not put religious trust in preaching to save?

Can one throw himself into the role or the institution which is his particular chosen form of ministry fully aware that it is only a particular and imperfect expression of that ministry, yet not be inhibited by that awareness from committing himself totally and enthusiastically to it? Can he prepare and preach his sermons with total discipline and wholehearted verve and without a regretful reservation, just as though his preaching were about to bring in the kingdom; yet at the same time can he be so unregretfully aware that his preaching is not about to bring in the kingdom that he is willing and able to recognize all the signs that may come his way that he needs to modify his preaching or even give it up in favor of the greater claims of another role? Can he thoroughly abandon himself and his qualms in the unreserved service of his preaching at the same time that he is prepared, when need be, to abandon this same preaching? Can he let himself go to his preaching without becoming so enslaved to it that he cannot let it go when need be? This is freedom of investment.

Such freedom can be contradicted in two ways. One is slavish addiction to the partial. The other is slavish devotion to the ultimate. The first treats the partial—in this case the preaching—as though it were the ultimate toward which it points and as though it were deserving of ultimate and absolute commitment. This contradiction to freedom seeks justification, righteousness, and fulfillment in terms of the discernible and readily verified good works and in terms of fidelity to specific obligations. This is the needful addiction against which Paul and Luther most leaned in their hymns to Christian freedom. The other contradiction to freedom is in the fearful inhibition to investment and commitment, which refuses to recognize the degree to which the ultimate is in the particular and holds out for that which can never be, the pure expression of the ultimate.

THE BONDAGE OF OVERINVESTMENT IN PARTICULARS

There is a kind of bondage to preaching—as to any other role or form of ministry—which is a self-investment so thorough that it is more than investment and becomes self-identification. Preaching becomes important not as *an* expression of ministry and of self but as *the* expression of ministry and of self. Techniques of exegesis and of voice, of construction and of delivery, effects in the pulpit and on people become not only cultivated and mastered, they become relied on—exclusively—as the means and as the evidence of faithfulness in vocation. Because the minister and ministry find their center, their justification, indeed the basis for their being in the activity of preaching—rather than in the fuller apprehension of ministry which preaching partly expresses and to which it points—one must unquestioningly serve and defend this activity as though *it* were the saving faith—which, in fact, it is for such persons. Competing claims on time and energy must be firmly set aside. Evidence of the need for other forms of ministry must be steadfastly overlooked. Signs that preaching, or one's own preaching in particular, is not having the effect one "believes in" must be resolutely denied.

The preaching role by which one feels justified must itself be justified by extension into and domination of all roles and relationships. Since one is not a minister who preaches or a Christian who preaches, or a man who preaches, but *is* a preacher, this must be clearly affirmed to self and to others at every opportunity. So that when one seeks him for personal counsel, is visited in the hospital, sits with him in a committee meeting or beside him at worship, one still must be made aware in tone and theme that here is the preacher. Such a minister is not free to minister or in the long run even to preach, because he is in bondage to his preaching, a bondage fashioned of exclusive reliance on it for definition and justification of self and of vocation.

There are ministers who similarly are in bondage to techniques and styles of personal counseling, administrative chores, one or another forms of direct social action, denominational committee structures, small group leadership, etc. Or perhaps the truer picture for most ministers is one of multiple and shifting bondages.

This is a kind of hot bondage, to be distinguished from the cool bondage to be described next, which is an avoidance of any investment, a refusal to identify ministry with any particular form or activity. On the face of it, one seems about as different from the other as manic exuberance does from depressive withdrawal. But the bondage is the same, because in neither instance is the minister (like either the manic or the depressive patient) free to pursue ministry as circumstances and his calling may require. The two forms of bondages may be similarly rooted (just as the manic's overlust for life and the depressive's withdrawal from life may be both rooted in a profound absence of self-esteem): Both forms of bondage may be the most satisfactory expressions of vocation a minister can make in the absence of a convincing confidence that he and his vocation are thoroughly grounded in that more ultimate support and direction which can be apprehended in but not identified with any particular expression. (And if most ministers are afflicted with the absence of firm faith, that may be why most ministers are in one or another kind of bondage. To that end, the more sermonic chapters are addressed, accompanying these analytic chapters.)

The persons introspective and searching enough to be reading this kind of book are not likely to be afflicted with this kind of hot bondage of super self-investment in one of the particulars of ministry. In fact, they are already all too aware of the perils of this kind of bondage. They can draw the portrait and make the accusation fully as sharply as I have. Perhaps they have been nodding their heads in full agreement over my characterization and recalling men whose ministries they can not admire precisely for the reasons I have described. This sensitivity to the perils of such bondage feeds whatever inclination they already have to avoid self-investment, precisely because such a self-investment is so risky.

THE BONDAGE
OF UNDER-INVESTMENT

This book is not primarily addressed to those suffering the addiction of over-investment. It is addressed to those suffering the bondage of cool under-investment. This too *is* a bondage, all the more so for being more readily recognized as such by those caught in it. If the other is something like the bondage of a prison, severely restricting the range of one's activities, this is more like the bondage of a ball and chain. One can adjust to being in a prison and come to accept its limits with the illusion that all of life is contained within them. A ball and chain which inhibits every step, maybe even the first step, is painfully recognizable. It may be especially painful just because or when one is not in a prison and has full view with no visible barriers over the vast terrain he would cover—deterred only by the weight that keeps him from getting started in any direction. Yet this bondage is, in an important sense, of our own choosing. And so are the strategies we adopt to preserve the bondage—games ministers play to keep cool.

Spokesman for the ultimate as a way of preserving links with it. This sense of keeping cool, on the verge, inhibited from involvement is usually recognized, lamented over, and suffered as a bondage by those caught in it. Only in some versions does it become denied and assume the form of a pompous and pretentious self-righteousness. Then from his pure podium or pedestal, one tries to make a virtue or a self-justification, out of his cool aloofness and noninvolvement. He flays at those captured in hot bondage. He dramatizes the imperfections and limitations of any particular involvement. Indeed such prophetic criticism of the prophets or of the preachers or of anyone else invested in any particular ministry is one of the ways he demonstrates his bondage. He must identify himself with that which is ultimate and perfect and on which he can safely depend and from which he must not move. If the captive described above finds his justification and assurance in clinging to a particular form, the captive here described finds himself and his vocation justified and assured only when he can link them immediately and unmistakably with the ultimate. Criticism of the imperfections and the approximations of the particular expressions is one way that he can identify himself with those more ultimate criteria which generate these criticisms.

This maneuver may be like that of the child who comes to feel himself assured of being on the same side as his parents by internalizing their standards and enforcing them, on himself and on others. Scolding himself or others may be a sure means of earning or fantasying parental favor. If this maneuver in bondage *is* similar to the process by which the superego becomes generated as a gigantic defensive maneuver to assure the goodwill of parents, this is not likely to be a coincidence. As the last chapter will suggest, it is entirely possible that in dealing with ministers we are often dealing with persons who *are* particularly dependent on such sources of support and well-being as parents represent, who are particularly likely to adopt such strategies to guarantee their support, and indeed who may have been particularly well practiced in just this process.

Mystical direct access. Perhaps the desire for direct access and relationship with the ultimate is almost a desire to sit on the lap of the ultimate or to hold the ultimate in one's own lap or one's pocket. Again, the analogy of regression to childhood may be more than analogy. One path of direct access may be through one or another form of mystical search and ascetic withdrawal from the particulars of the world.

Aloofness from involvement to preserve purity. But above all, the chief strategy—at least the one of most concern in this book—for avoiding alienation from the ultimate is the strategy of avoiding any particular investment. To invest oneself, as in preaching, is to expose oneself to the criticisms which inevitably accrue to a particular investment. It is precisely the person most dependent on the ultimate who is also most likely to have internalized the ultimate's criteria by which the particular is judged partial. In other words, it is precisely the person who most needs to feel close to the ultimate who will be most aware of how any particular investment alienates him from it. He is also most aware of how any one investment, as in preaching, separates him from those other expressions of the ultimate in other particulars, as in other forms of ministry. This inability to invest oneself in the particular, because of the alienation from the ultimate it seems to imply, may or may not be accomplished by one of the other strategies for identifying with the ultimate—being spokesman for the ultimate, or mystic seeker of direct access.*

---

* Another strategy is to try to go out on several limbs simultaneously. This is called dialectic or paradox or something of this sort and is very popular in seminaries. Another strategy popular in intellectual circles is to stand back and analyze the whole dilemma—as this book is doing—giving one the feeling, as it were, of standing beside God, watching it all.

Theologians encouraging frozen bondage. Perhaps it is the business of a theologian always to be the spokesman for the transcendent and to remind us how limited and partial is our investment in any particular ideal or action or role. But it does seem remarkable how common, and perhaps more importantly, how popular are the men and the slogans which, in warning us from overinvestment in the particular, have the effect of anchoring us so firmly we make no investment. Thus we are directed to *ultimate* concerns and to the God beyond any gods we may possibly know (Tillich); we are urged to a *radical* monotheism (H. R. Niebuhr) and an *absolute* dependence (Schleiermacher); we find the age's most systematic theology grounded in a Christology which is criterion for all but which eludes ordinary definition and apprehension (Barth); we are guided in the grand hermeneutical task of demythologizing or otherwise finding the kernel of kerygma which has been so wrapped over with husks (Bultmann); but every attempt to express the kernel is judged to be only another husk. And the secular theologies and secular ministers, too, generate their thrust from the critique of the existing and traditional religious forms on behalf of a still more ultimate. But that more ultimate criterion somehow consistently eludes statement—perhaps in defensive recognition that statement of the ultimate criterion will render it vulnerable to the same judgment.

How cool bondage feels. If the captive in hot bondage seems preoccupied with the techniques of sermon construction and delivery, so may this cool captive, but for different reasons. The former is preoccupied because satisfactory performance supports his feeling of well-being. The latter is more likely to be anxiously forestalling poor performance. He identifies with the ultimate values and criteria by imposing them, in advance, on his own behavior.* The impos-

---

* Another basis for the cool bondage may be the desire to avoid

sible ideal of an absolutely perfect sermon is too much before him, and he cannot venture a word without recognizing how far short he falls. So too he is particularly alerted to the disapproval of his hearers, or perhaps their fawning approval for what he knows all too well are the wrong reasons. Words come slowly in preparation and subdued in delivery. Investment in each word is almost too risky to warrant spontaneous flow or forceful enthusiasm, for each word may be the wrong word, or at the very least, precludes others. A sentence is hardly begun before a dozen necessary qualifications flood the mind. One illustration or analogy is hardly fashioned before the mind is flooded with all the ways it fails to fit. And all of the attention and effort these misgivings compel only enhance the agony, because they make the minister work harder on the sermon, take it more seriously, give it more refined attention than he knows it deserves. His difficulties in investing himself force him to invest himself more in the preaching than he can find comfortable or justified. Choice of topic and text, organization and development, style of delivery—everything becomes a matter of uncertain conviction, because of uncertain commitment. He cannot commit himself to the form of preaching, or to any of its forms, because to do so risks alienation from that which he would express and foster with his preaching.

But here is the final despair and irony. To be loyal to his ultimate purposes of ministry, he cannot invest himself adequately in any expression of ministry. But this inability, on behalf of the ultimate purposes of his ministry, is precisely

---

the test. A minister may be living with the conviction—which allies him with the ultimate—that he potentially can act in faithfulness to the criteria of the ultimate. Others may flounder because of their alienation, but he is the "good boy" (and perhaps also the effective one) whose actions would not be tainted—if and when he chose to act. He *can* make the particular faithful to the ultimate. He can live with this conviction, and derive the reassurance it yields so long—and he secretly knows only so long—as he does not put it to the test of action.

what sabotages his loyalty to the transcendent. The absence of a vigorous style or of any style at all annuls his communication from the pulpit. So does his very inability to take a single idea and, leaving aside the many qualifications and the many companion ideas, to develop it vigorously and thoroughly. Because he cannot comfortably preach with particulars and in partialness, he cannot preach at all the important truths in whose name he abstains from partial and limited statement.

FREEDOM

But there is also a kind of freedom of investment. Here is the minister who throws himself into his preaching—or any other activity—with all the vigor and enthusiasm and verve of the first "hot" captive above. But he knows just as well as the second "cool" captive how wrong and partial it can be. So he is as free to abandon or correct or try again his preaching as he is to venture it.

Somehow—and though this "somehow" requires considerable development, I can defer it to later pages and refuse to be inhibited by this fact from trying to state my present point as clearly as possible—this minister finds his self and his vocation centered, assured, and justified, on some reliable basis. This leaves him freed from the need to find his justification either by exclusive and blind reliance on a particular form of preaching or by the elusive and yearning search for an immediate and direct encounter with the saving and directing ultimate truth. In short, he has been freed for investment because he has been able to find a mediative experience of redemption and/or of call. He can trust the mediation for that which it mediates without confusing it with that which it mediates. He is able to invest himself into preaching, and into preaching with a particular style and with a particular topic with particular words to particular people in a particular place, with all the commitment and vigor *as though* it were a kind of pure instance of undiluted ministry. Yet at the same time he knows, as a kind of secret divine joke, that this is not so and that he is treating it only "as though" it were.

Let us illustrate this general notion of freedom by considering some very concrete and particular incidents that might arise in preaching. Let us consider three kinds of "disasters" which may be yielded by investment in a sermon, to see what response to the disaster distinguishes between the minister in bondage and the minister who has invested himself in freedom.

How he deals in freedom with an analogy gone astray. Suppose he works hard to develop a theological point with an analogy concerning the relations between parents and children. If someone's after-the-sermon narthex reaction is to quarrel with his theory of child-raising, he will not deny and overlook the failure of communication (as would the first captive, who might simply pass over the remark with a kind of jovial "I'm glad you were listening so carefully," or else find ways to misconstrue it as some kind of development of the point he did want to make). Nor will the freely invested minister be surprised or disheartened, as would the second captive, that his best efforts have missed the point and have raised a tangential response. In the first place, he is not so dependent on evidences of effect and effectiveness that he is forced to believe the effects of the sermon are limited to and measurable by just such reactions. But neither is he so dependent on the sermon he preached that he is afraid to follow, closely and with new investment, this new prospect of ministry now offered to him. What may possibly be so important about child-rearing practices in the life of this parishioner that the question erupts and interrupts in this way? This may well be a new occasion for ministry. Or what was there about the original point that drove the parishioner to the evasive action of discussing the analogy? Perhaps the sermon registered more keenly than he can admit, and here is the point for needed future ministry. Or perhaps the analogy is all the parishioner can understand, and there is a lesson for the minister to learn about how well he is getting his main points across. Wherever the parishioner's remarks may lead, the minister is free to follow, not bound by his past investment in the sermon.

Part of the reason the minister does not despair over having worked so hard on the analogy only to have its point lost is his awareness that only by developing the analogy as fully as he did could he have provoked this kind of response. His investment has borne fruit, even though in an unanticipated form. In the half-invested captivity that might have resulted from his anticipation of the analogy's failure, he would have developed the illustration so timidly that it might well have not seemed real enough and vivid enough either to carry his own point or to provoke the tangential concerns of the parishioner.

But as fully as he may invest himself in these new occasions of ministry, he is free to abandon them too. The parishioner's question may not be revealing matters of great moment, or it may be touching on matters too tender for further exposure at this point. Maybe he is only making conversation. In following this new lead seriously and with commitment, the minister is not so bound to it, so hoping for results, so needing to use his counseling skills and psychological insights, so eager to improve his next sermon, that he cannot cheerfully and freely abandon this lead too.

How he deals in freedom with disagreement. Suppose a preacher feels called to try to interpret to his people the Black Power sentiments of the inner-city residents. And suppose this evokes an angry response from a parishioner who is part of the city government and sees his own earnest efforts to improve the ghetto simply thwarted by the stubborn intransigence of the Black Power leaders. The first captive would be likely to deny the contradiction and confrontation. He might dismiss the man and his contention as provincial or misguided or otherwise not really in a position to offer valid challenge to that position in which he has invested himself. Or he might accomplish the same purpose by developing the kind of personal and jovial rapport with the man which "transcends" the challenge by not taking him seriously.

The second kind of captive, if he had indeed achieved this much investment as to have preached a provocative sermon, would be likely to view the reaction with despair ("Here I can't even register my point with the man it is most important to reach.") and derive from the episode a lesson not to risk such forthright investment again.

The freed minister may celebrate the fact that he has so vigorously thrown himself into a real issue as to provoke this kind of reaction. But he is also ready to abandon the terms of his statement and take up the matter afresh in terms and with the person as it now presents itself. The new need to minister may be related to (even disclosed by), but be different from, the need for ministry the sermon was intended to address. What do the Black Power leaders and principles mean to *this man* in his particular occupation? This is a new and perhaps urgent matter which may also require a great deal of new investment by the minister to pursue. What sort of frustrations or competitiveness does this man feel? How has he come to interpret his own vocation in a way that requires him to feel the neighborhood leadership as competitive rather than as a potential extension of his vocational aims? How can the purposes of the Black Power leaders be meaningfully interpreted to this particular man? These may be the kinds of questions which can now be fruitfully employed. Or perhaps others. Or perhaps none. At any rate the freed minister stands ready to invest his efforts in the particular forms in which they may present themselves on the particular occasion.

Out on a limb proving God. Take the case of a minister who preached on Pentecost, fervently wanting to emphasize the divine foundations of the church and the consequent scope of its mission. He dramatized all the seeming super-natural elements in the second chapter of Acts, especially the multiple languages, reminding his listeners of how much trouble they had—without God—in learning even one additional language. He pointed out that crowds normally are hostile to such "street-corner preaching," dramatizing instances of this in the congregation's own town, and argued that the receptive response to Peter's sermon proved divine intervention. He made the same argument for the assembly of people from distant cities, contending that without divine intervention such diverse aliens in a strange city would have clustered with their own kind and not come together in one place. He even produced a map suggesting that all the cities represented by Peter's hearers formed a kind of a star, which seemed to be still additional evidence of supernatural warrant. He emphasized the careful construction and subtly effective strategy of Peter's sermon, again arguing that only with divine intervention could such a refined sermon be preached by such an oaf as we otherwise know Peter to be. In short, he combed through the account of Pentecost to read in it every possible basis of inference of divine intervention—and maybe even some that were not so possible. He was determined to prove his point. He impulsively and heedlessly invested himself in it. He went way out on a limb.

After the sermon his people called him on it. "Who wound you up today?" "You forgot to say that people came from fifteen locations. That's the five letters in Peter's name multiplied by the three letters in God." "I was willing to believe you when you started out."

He acknowledges the jibes. "I was on a rampage, wasn't I?" "OK, I'll use that bit about the fifteen locations next week." "So I should have quit while I was ahead." He did register a few dos and don'ts to follow in his future preaching. More significant evidence of his freedom, the following week he began his sermon with a caricature of the preceding week, using the divine multiplication problem his parishioner had ironically suggested. Having conceded in this way his single-track, determined effort to invest the church with sanctions, he reflected with them on the implications of such an effort. Did his exegetical dredging betray some doubt on his part as to whether the church *is* God's institution? Perhaps; he confessed to occasional doubts and despair. He thought it more likely represented the earnestness of his own conviction that the church is God's, combined with the frustration he felt in stating this clearly and convincingly to the congregation. Then with this frustration acknowledged, he ventured to suggest the various possible bases for commitment to the church as God's institution. He discussed with them the kinds of criteria they might look for in their own church for discovering whether it seemed to represent God's purposes.

Compare this "freed" minister's experience with the kinds of bondage described above. The second "cool" kind of captive would never have gone so far in relentlessly pursuing a single line of thought as the Pentecost sermon—and he therefore would never have gotten beyond it into the fresher and richer insights provoked by it. He would have been locked behind misgivings over venturing specific interpretations. The images of professors back in seminary or critics in his congregation would have hovered over his shoulder, inhibiting any such untoward expression with masses of qualifications, interpretations of the interpretations, and a thoroughly balanced and discreet presentation.

The first kind of captive would have so needed the point he was making and/or his sense of effectiveness in making it that he could never have entertained or acknowledged the rejoinders. He would long since have signaled to his people the rigid needfulness of his investment in his sermons, so they would not have ventured to reply so directly and productively. They would have protested more indirectly—in not discussing the sermon at all with him in the narthex, in dropping out from Sunday morning worship, perhaps in a discreet, timid inquiry as to other interpretations of Acts 2.

He could not have come close to seeing these as comments on his sermon and would have tried to respond to these rejoinders in some other terms: in frustration or with cajoling over their unresponsiveness to sermon and to worship, perhaps welcoming the inquiry in interpretation as evidence of an interested convert to his viewpoint. "While Peter got three thousand people asking what they should do next; I'm glad that I got at least one."

The freed investor described in the incident could thoroughly throw himself into an idea and an argument that must have seemed to him at the time as reasonable and appropriate.* But he also could transcend and not be bound to this argument, evidenced by the good humor by which he entertains and apparently welcomes responses, evidenced also by his willingness and ability to profit and correct his understanding of what was realistic and appropriate, but evidenced most of all in his ability to work through the encounter and come out the other side with richer insights.

SOURCES OF FREEDOM

What can account for the difference between bondage and freedom? What differences in experiences, attitudes, outlooks, self-understandings, could there be between the minister who is enslaved in either kind of bondage and the minis-

---

* The free use of largely inappropriate material in the Pentecost sermon of this example raises one form of the persistent problem of freedom and responsibility. The resolution depends, in this instance, on a distinction between internalized discipline and outer constraints. We can celebrate a minister's freedom in vigorously pursuing his ideas at whatever stage they have evolved, while still regretting the unsoundness of the ideas. The freedom consists in the full self-investment, unattenuated by anticipation of others' constraints. The unsoundness has reference to the internalized criteria invoked in developing the material invested in. When these internal bases for judgment are deficient, they are more likely to be remedied through the free confrontation described here—indeed the minister in this instance ends the episode with sounder bases for judgment—than through a timid inhibition which keeps them secret and not subject to correction.

ter who has the freedom to invest himself? The customary answer pointed to by the combined weight of our theological and psychological heritage is almost cliché—but we ought not to be intimidated by that either into a fear of restating it: The minister who can feel assured that his life and his vocation are supported, guaranteed, warranted, accepted, thoroughly rooted and allied with—in the economy of the biblical language, "justified by"—that which is truly the center and ground of life and ministry and capable of providing such justification. This is the man who is free to invest himself because he is free to abandon his investment. He has no need for the kind of self-justification which comes from clinging desperately and blindly to particular accomplishments and investments, nor for the self-justification that comes from clinging desperately and blindly to direct, immediate, and unmistakable evidence of belonging to the ultimate. If a man had firm religious faith, he would be free to function more effectively as a minister. If a man felt assured of the unconditional unquestioning support of persons important to him (be they parents, parishioners, or others), he would be freed.

Such statements are true. But they are indeed so commonly and easily stated that they carry little meaning. What actual experience might such statements point to? What is this trust, which makes all the difference? And where does it come from? The last chapter will attempt to give these statements some objective content by suggesting actual biographical events which are likely to lead to the trust that makes possible a ministry of freedom. It will venture to distinguish these experiences in the life history from those that are more likely to lead to the fearful mistrust that generates a ministry of bondage. The remaining section of this chapter will attempt, largely analogically and subjectively, some understanding of this experience of trust, for which the last chapter will suggest antecedents. What experience or understanding of himself might a Christian be referring to if he says he feels an unconditional support and assurance which frees him to venture risky investments, risky vocational investments and—if there is in fact a distinction—risky self-investments.

What is the confidence that permits him to go out on a limb? We use the imagery of the risky limb to distinguish among several things he might mean. And we use the distinctions to suggest that some possible meanings are more faithful than others to the traditional Christian understanding of trust and its resulting freedom.

Guaranteed soft landing. One might mean that he trusts himself on a limb which may break off because he feels sure that a soft landing is guaranteed him, even if it does break. This is a kind of religious faith which can be called *compensating,* and has also been called *illusory* by many. It is a faith which looks *outside* any present moment of involvement, whatever its possible risks, for a compensating satisfaction or affirmation. Heaven-imagery is one version of such a compensating faith. So is the retreat, or prospect of retreat, into a moralistic self-satisfaction or a mutually congratulatory in-group. It is the freedom a small boy has to provoke the bully of the streets, knowing that if his bluff is called, he can run back into his yard, shut the gates, and count on the support of mother or father. Here is the academic freedom of the professor on tenure. He can venture risky causes and risky ideas, because they do not risk his job. He is guaranteed his "chair."

Any of the ministers described above as free enough to risk an investment in his preaching might derive this freedom from his confidence that important personal supports are guaranteed apart from and regardless of his preaching. "Important personal supports" might be external, perhaps God's goodwill and his personal religious salvation, perhaps the love of his wife, his mother, or his parishioners, or perhaps the endorsement of his ministry by his professors back at school, or his fellow ministers, or his bishop. Such support is offered "unconditionally," or more likely, based on conditions other than his preaching performance (his sense of God's goodwill, perhaps, based on his virtuous personal and devotional life; his wife's love, perhaps based on personal characteristics more apparent at home than in the pulpit; his bishop's approval, perhaps based on limited institutional criteria, etc.). Important personal supports might be more internal. Perhaps his self-confidence and his vocation derive from the competence he feels in some other role than preaching. He might regard himself primarily as a counselor or social actionist or community leader or discussion leader and see these as separate enough from preaching that risking the latter does not really threaten the self-assurance based on the former. He is free to feel abandon in, or to abandon, preaching because his self- and vocational assurance is elsewhere.

This type of compensating faith undoubtedly works. It does yield this kind of freedom for segments of life and for vocations which can be sufficiently isolated so that disaster in the segment does not seem to threaten disaster to the life or to the vocation. This way of understanding the relation of faith and freedom is undoubtedly a common pattern among religious persons. It is a pattern which has been made particularly popular in recent years when the analogy of a psychotherapist's acceptance has been used to understand the dynamics of faith: The therapist can supply a freeing, virtually unconditional acceptance (as a patient's parents often have not) because the therapist is isolated in the patient's life and is not threatened or, for that matter, even affected by misdeeds or deficiences of the patient (as parents were not immune).

This way of gaining assurance and freedom may be common, effective, religious, and even psychologically understandable. But is it Christian? And, is it thoroughly and effectively freeing? As the pattern is applied to God, it assumes a nurturing God who is remote from the actual affairs of men, and unaffected by them, and unsuffering with them. It assumes a God who is, like the nurturant mother, waiting for her young refugee from street brawls, protected and protecting behind the garden gate and off the street. It assumes a God, who, like a psychotherapist, conducts an hour of sanctuary once a week or once a day, remote and essentially unaffected by the affairs of the rest of the week.

This pattern of thought assumes a view of self and vocation in which fragmentation and isolation is possible. In the example before us, preaching can be entered into freely—and even, perhaps, lightly and irresponsibly—just because it is seen separated from the crucial sectors of one's life and vocation. This compartmentalization is alien to the Christian's understanding of the integrity of life afforded by the Creator God, and to the integrity of his own response to the calls of that God. In the last analysis, such a basis for freedom is not that of a risky investment of self, because the self is not invested or risked. Such freedom is possible only on the edges of life.

Cling to the guaranteed limb. Another way to understand the assurance that gives freedom is to understand the assurance as guaranteed, as it were, for certain limbs. The risk is in choosing the limb, for some limbs do break off. But if one does select the "right" limb, and if he can find evidence assuring himself that the limb is guaranteed, then he can experience the confidence and the resulting freedom. Here is the pietistic confidence in vocation and institutional structure so long as vocation and structure bear identifiable marks of being "true." So long as one can point to the evidence that he has chosen and performed faithfully, the covenant assures that God will provide. Here the childhood analogy is not that one can run to an ever-available supporting mother, nor that one can guarantee nonalienation from parents by internalizing their sanctions. But here the analogy is that one can guarantee parental approval and the sense of nonalienation by performing those particular behaviors which they are known to endorse and sanction: get good grades, don't smoke, brush your teeth, fasten your seat belt.

The preacher might be assured by memories of his seminary professors' instructions, by the unexpected ingenious interpretations he finds for the text, by the smoothness with which the idea develops, or by other signs he may interpret as ratifying his enterprise—with a confidence that he is on the right track. Hence he can pursue it freely, heedless of more routine cautions and risks.

This view too is common, psychologically understandable, and religious. But again there is question as to how Christian it is and how really effective. This too assumes a compartmentalization which breeds irresponsibility. It assumes a bargaining God and almost a finite God who rules over some segments of life, but not others. It assumes a God somehow unrelated to the risks and the defeats of most men in most areas of life. Again there is a real question as to how much self is invested and how much risk.

Freedom as obligation. There is another basis for understanding free and risky investment which is not unknown. This is to regard freedom as a kind of duty. We have learned that real faith is supposed to generate freedom. If such freedom is the hallmark of faith, then one ought to demonstrate his faith by gritting his teeth, rolling up his sleeves, and forging ahead in earnest freedom. One goes out on the limb because it is the thing to do. Here is the child of the enlightened parents, struggling fiercely to be spontaneous and creative, because this is what they want for him—unlike the "unenlightened" parents who insist on neatness. Here is the compulsively rebellious adolescent, determined to demonstrate his freedom.

But such "freedom" as this partakes of a grim lawfulness and calculation which itself contradicts freedom. Acting the role of the freed man does not induce the spirit of freedom but only locks one into the role, rigidly. One responds to the preconception of what freedom is like and to the sanctions that enforce it, not to whatever new occasions may present themselves and beckon free creative pursuit. One goes out on the limb because the going out is important, not because the limb is important.

Assurance is in the breaking. In none of the above understandings is there revealed clear understanding of a redeemer God who acts in the midst of rupture and alienation—the breaking off of limbs. But now we consider that freedom of the man who moves out on a limb not *in spite of* the possibility it may break off, but *because of* it. One moves freely into risks and crisis because he knows that in—and perhaps only in—crisis and disaster is there prospect of new revelation and new creation and new relation. We have learned that one is most loyal to the creative potentialities within himself and within others when he ventures beyond the confines and into the risky. Adam and Eve did not really become selves and neither do children until they risk exercise of the freedom which is theirs. Even when the risk turns out badly, as apparently it often does, there is still more real selfhood—which is itself a kind of faithfulness to the Creator God—than without the risk.

Here too is a cliché, an apocalyptic and existential cliché. What content can it have? One analogy is with the child finding himself punished by his parents, who also finds that this punishment does not jeopardize the relationship with the parents, but builds new relationship. The punishment itself is something they want to and do share with him, to talk about, to reflect about, to interpret; in *this* sharing is a renewed and vitalized relationship and support, firmer and more intimate than that broken by the punishment and the misbehavior which produced it. Yet without having ventured in the old relationship to the point of punishment there would not have been the new to share.

Another analogy is the psychotherapy patient who ventures to expose himself to the point at which anxiety and dread take over and he must balk at further self-disclosure and display what the therapist will know as resistance.

But the resistance becomes the focus of the psychotherapy, the promise of dynamic engagements, the basis for therapeutic progress; if the patient never resisted, the therapy hour would go smoothly, and the therapy would make no progress.

Or it is like the married couple who venture to expose themselves in increasing intimacy of relationship, knowing they are leading themselves to friction and failure yet knowing that in sharing this friction and failure—if they can—there will be keener intimacy and trust than would ever be possible without it.

It is when the religious pilgrim ventures beyond the comfortable and into the risky and real grappling with faith that he is eventually driven to the despair and breaking point "Lord, I believe, help thou my unbelief." The Christian—the follower of the cross—is freed to risk because he knows that help comes especially at the breaking point.

From this point of view the preacher is free to throw himself unreservedly into his preaching not because he feels confident of being spared catastrophe if the sermon fails but because he has the confidence that maturity of faith and self and ministry—for himself and for his congregation—lies in working through the catastrophe. He fully develops his insights with all the energy and verve and resources and talents he can muster and hopes the congregation can respond in equal freedom. In this encounter may be disaster, and beyond the disaster, growth. The examples above have suggested three instances in which this can happen.

ADMINISTRATION VS. MINISTRY

Administrative work is the bane of ministry, by most accounts. It is, as ministers often see it, the unwelcome and unmanageable burden they carry that retards the progress of their ministry as they want to pursue it. Ministers report themselves caught in administrative work when they want to be in ministry. When ministers are asked what part of their work they most enjoy or think most important, they mention pastoral, or preaching, or teaching activities first, and administration comes last. But when they are asked how they actually spend their time, administration comes a clear first, and the others lag behind. This is the often replicated finding of research studies. The dilemma becomes more poignant and more urgent when we hear individual ministers tell of their despair*; or when we see men leaving the administratively burdened parish for what seems to be purer (i.e., administration-free) forms of ministry in teaching, in hospital chaplaincy, or in such secularized forms as psychotherapist, social worker, or politician; or when we see the restiveness elevated and rationalized as an elaborate critique of the institutionalized structures because they blur vision, drain talent, and inhibit ministry.

---

* For example: "I wanted to develop a meaningful program and close pastoral relations. And I could have. But we all got bogged down in the machinery of the church. Like quicksand, it just sucks you in. You can't help yourself."

TWO KINDS OF TASKS

The conflict between administration and the purposes of ministry is most often expressed as a competition for time, effort, and energy between two kinds of tasks: A minister feels led by his call, his training, his personal preferences, the expectations of his seminary mentors, and his assessment of the needs of his people to devote himself to pastoral, preaching, or teaching activities. He wants to do those things which will advance his people's Christian growth, make them more forcefully to know the assurances and demands of God. But once actually on the job, he feels compelled to invest himself heavily in administrative activities: recruiting, organizing, chairing, deciding, planning, arranging. At telephone, at dictating machine, over coffee, in office, in study, and in living room, he is doing all the things required to initiate and maintain activities and organization, and not performing ministry.

What prompts this attention to administrative tasks is not always clear. The minister often reports it as deriving from demands alien to his own purposes: from the expectations of superiors, or of his constituents in the congregation, or from the autonomous requirements of the institution itself, an institution which somehow seems a necessary but not entirely integrated adjunct to the ministry he would pursue.

But it is also possible that the impetus to administration comes from within. It simply may be inherent in the minister's prime objectives. (Even pastoral counseling interviews and Bible study groups and picket lines have to be scheduled.) Or there may be something inherently (though unconsciously) attractive about these administrative tasks themselves, perhaps because they are more easily defined and provide more obvious evidence of achievement, perhaps because they provide relieving surcease from the more demanding tasks.

In any case, whether the so-called "role conflict" is between the minister and others, or is within the minister himself, it is usually defined as a conflict between two different kinds of tasks, administrative vs. ministry.

TWO STYLES OF MINISTRY

But even though they talk about the conflict in terms of time and effort, they may often mean more than that. It may be that ministers experience the conflict more keenly and more deeply not merely as a conflict between two different kinds of tasks, but as a conflict between two different *ways* of doing the same tasks.

Administering vs. pastoring. A minister who lists pastoral activity as first choice among his possible roles may be ready to tell us—if he were given a different kind of questionnaire that permitted him to do so—that he wants to have a kind of pastoral attitude and approach about all his ministry. He wants to *be* a pastor, whatever he may be *doing*. He may mean he wants to approach all his personal relationships and each of his various activities with a freedom and a joy, an acceptance and a concern for others which he finds a particularly effective expression of the gospel, a particularly effective ministry. A minister may find it especially easy to express this ministry in relatively formal situations of counseling, but to be a pastor may mean to express this attitude with his parish and his parishioners in whatever activity.

But he feels this pastoral stance contradicted by an administrative stance that he unwillingly and unintentionally finds himself drawn into. This conflict, between two different styles of functioning, saps away his sense of vocational integrity and personal fulfillment. Instead of being concerned about persons for their sake, and instead of putting himself in their service, he finds himself treating them in relation to his purposes, and his institution's. The I–Thou relation he intends becomes contradicted by the I–It relation he finds himself pursuing. Instead of entering into their lives

104

and ministering to *their* troubles, he finds himself asking them to enter into his concerns (as promoter and guardian of the institution) and to help to solve *his* problems. Instead of expressing trust and freedom, he shows himself fretful, concerned for results and calculating how to achieve them. Instead of evidencing the faith and confidence in healing resources available to all men from outside of themselves, he finds himself trusting himself, his own diagnosis, analysis, prescription, manipulation. Instead of being free and open, he is calculating and controlling.

How can he be two things to the same people? How can he be two kinds of person himself? How can he plan successfully to recruit a Sunday school teacher, at the same time he tries to be open and helpful toward the needs and plights of her life. When she reports the plights in her life as part of the reason for declining the Sunday school class, what does a minister then respond to, her needs or the Sunday school's? How does he develop his relationship with her, with what ends in view and with what style—as an administrator and salesman, or as a pastor and healer? He can hardly be both things to her.

How can he be permissive and understanding toward the natural expressions of the teen-agers in his church, at the same time that he is responsibly aware of the "organizational problems" occasioned by the footprints they leave on the wall of the room the women's society has just redecorated.

How can he lead his deacons to understand the freedom and grace in the gospel in the devotional part of their monthly meeting, and, later, worry with them about the procedures of the communion service or urge them to more conscientious parish calling?

Even scheduling the next session with a counselee requires an attention to detail and conscientious and skillful problem-solving that may violate precisely the spirit of freedom one tries to create within the counseling session: "Well, if you find that your baby-sitter can't be there at 2:45, call me and I'll see if I can change my 4:00 appointment to 3:00. But I won't be able to let you know until about noon that day, because the 4:00 person is out of town until that morning. If that won't work, I'll try to come out to your house so that you won't need a baby-sitter, if I can finish the luncheon meeting early enough so that I can get out to your house and we can have a good talk and I can still get back to the church by 4:00."

A pastor is a shepherd, but the image is ambiguous. Is a shepherd one who risks his life to find the one lost lamb? Or is the shepherd the one who, with his dog and staff, herds his sheep along the path he has chosen for them to follow?

Pope John XXIII explicitly announced the "pastor" as the controlling image of his reign. The shepherd is a prominent image in the New Testament writings bearing the name he chose. But look what John XXIII did to the administrative structure. His pastoral pontificate had to be followed by an administrator, who made the preservation of the institution his keynote. We can have the two in sequence, but apparently—as any pastor knows—not simultaneously and in the same person.

Administering vs. arousing to mission. Another minister might put his prime goals differently but find them equally contradicted by the pressures to be an administrator. Rather than being pastor, he might most of all want to lead his people to the vision and to the willingness and freedom to extend their own self-investment into broader circles of need and life. He wants the affairs of the city and of the world to agitate them fully as much as the lunch-hour schedule in their children's school, the redecoration of their own home, or a successful fair at the church. Whether in the pulpit or committee meeting, in personal counseling or at a church dinner, his purpose is to enlarge his people's understanding of who they are and what they are expected to be. But how can he do these things when he is unavoidably the responsible administrative head of the quite local institution, the church. As with the pastor impeded by administration, the question is the same for this man: How can he be two things to the same people? How can he be two kinds of person himself? How can he be a symbol for the expansion of ego and concern when he is unmistakably the symbol for the local neighborhood institution which necessarily constricts investment of self.

How can he try to recruit a prospective Sunday school teacher with the argument or with the assumption that the education of the church's children has high priority at the same time that he wants to upset just such prevailing priorities held by this woman and others and expand their sensitivity to the needs of persons far beyond the confines of the parish. The dilemma is all the keener when he has chosen this prospective teacher precisely because she does have some sense of mission which he wants her to communicate to the children.

How can he organize a meeting to expand people's concern for housing needs in the city, when the very act of organizing the meeting and recruiting attendance inevitably implies a narrowing of focus on the importance of *this* meeting in this place—a claim symbolized by the fact that the minister *is* investing himself in the "administrative" chores of arranging this meeting rather than, in fact, in the broader mission he was directed toward.

And—the near-cliché dilemma—how can he, by word and deed, try to stretch his people's vision without risking loss of their hearing, loss of their participation in the occasions he can reach them, and loss of their support of the position from which he would speak and act? How can he minister to them without losing the opportunity to minister to them, except by careful and tedious administrative fence-building? How can he justify accommodating himself and his ministry to this need for fence-building, on their terms, without sacrificing too large a portion of that call to mission, which is the purpose of the whole thing?

CHOOSE WHICH MASTER

If administration and ministry contradict each other, then one must go. If the terms of the dilemma are those expressed above, then the prospects of "holding the two in productive tension" or any other compromise, seem doomed. The more plausible solution would seem a forthright choice. We see this choice made on every hand.

Some men choose administration. They choose to devote their efforts to administrative tasks, and they choose to "be" administrators in every role. In pastoral contacts they respond to personal need and personal difficulty with a calculating diagnostic action-oriented approach. They promote mission through administrative and political finesse, managing budgets, manipulating the right people into strategic positions. Most of us deplore this choice of administration over ministry. Perhaps we deplore it for good reasons: we may believe that pastoral and mission goals are hardly met unless persons' insights are deepened and expanded through more profound encounters than the administrative style permits. But we may often deplore the choice for administration on more primitive, prejudiced grounds: we are perhaps fundamentally suspicious of the kind of task and style which administration is, the routine, humdrum manipulation of the things and people of the world. We are predisposed to think that such fare simply is not exalted, magnificent enough to be allied with the purposes of the ministry as we see them.

Therefore the choice is more often made the other way. The dead weight of administration is sloughed off and pure ministry emerges. If it is the denominational tie which is blamed for the administration, then this is ruptured and a freer context sought. If it is the local church institution which is to be blamed, then this is to be forsaken. Pure pastoral ministry can be sought in a hospital chaplaincy and pure mission in the city redevelopment agency. Or even if the administrative tasks are retained, the administrative *style* can be renounced. Administrative tasks can be approached with a pastoral style. The administrative problems can be essentially ignored and become instead the occasion for establishing rapport and for exposing deeper levels of personality and personal relationship.

But perhaps the problems of administration need not and ought not to be put in terms of such a sharp polarity and disparity from other ministry. And perhaps the fact that the problem *is* so often put in terms of such polarity is another clue to the dilemma in which the minister finds himself.

ADMINISTRATION: STEREOTYPE AND SCAPEGOAT?

Ministers' antagonism to administration is often curiously extreme and vigorous, often with a relentless, heedless passion which would be called, if it were applied to a social group, a prejudice. The organizing, recruiting, planning, arranging, troubleshooting, and problem-solving activities of the minister are too seldom viewed rationally or carefully, to discover which are constructive and which are wasteful; instead they are most often lumped together under a single label—administration—with which they can be sneered at, dismissed, and blamed for failures of ministry. Whatever the large or small failure of ministry, administration is most often blamed. Whether in the privacy of his own brooding over less-than-ideal pastoral relationships, whether in the Monday luncheon group of ministers sharing frustration over failure to arouse people to a vigorous sense of mission, whether the frustration is escalated into an elaborate, highly rationalized critique of the structural facts of church life, these organizing, structuring activities are by far the most popular target. One is tempted to paraphrase Tertullian's account of the scapegoat persecution of the Christians.* Whenever

---

* "They take the Christians to be the cause of every disaster to the state, of every misfortune to the people. If the Tiber reaches the wall, if the Nile does not reach the fields, if the sky does not move, or if the earth does, if there is a famine, or if there is a plague, the cry is at once: 'The Christians to the lions.' "

books are unread, families estranged, sermons uninspiring, people not aroused to mission, laymen not elevated to theological literacy, the cry is always the same: "Send the administrative work to an assistant." Yet such scapegoating, such solution by segregation, always exposes the irrational prejudice that lies behind it. For getting rid of the alleged devil doesn't solve the problem it was blamed for. Disposing of the administrative tasks doesn't provide remedy for the deficiencies of ministry for which they are blamed. On the contrary, the facts seem to be that when administrative tasks are disposed of by redefining roles and restructuring organizations, by hiring secretaries and assistants, by abandoning organization, new impediments arise to take their place, and these, too, usually get branded "administrative." The solutions, whether reorganization or larger staff, tend to breed their own new and inevitably "administrative" demands. And each minister, as well as each book-writer, must finally face that moment of truth when he does succeed in carving out a morning or a month absolutely free of administrative demands or distractions. He discovers, far more often than not, that his aspirations, for ministry or for study, or for writing, remain unfulfilled and still victim of distractions; and for the responsibility for this he must look inward. More elaborate reforms in structure or changes in career intended to abolish or to obviate administrative drain on ministry, far more often than not prove equally illusory: house-churches, redevelopment agencies, hospital chaplaincies, merged parishes, hardly turn out to require less attention to organizational life, and somehow still don't bring in an age of pure ministry.

The preceding section has put the problem of administration as ministers usually put it, as a contradiction of ministry. I have explored this way of putting it as vigorously as possible, to see how much truth there is to such analysis. There is some. But—I now want to contend—there is not enough validity to this argument to warrant the frequency with which it is offered and the ease with which it is accepted. I now think the preceding is something approximating the rationalization of a prejudice. I have written it as conscientiously and rationally as possible. But in a rereading it seems strained, forced, over-rationalized: Recruiting a Sunday school teacher and organizing a discussion meeting don't really constrict and deny ministry *that* much; the two recent popes cannot be contrasted *that* sharply. Yet—I now submit—these strains go more easily undetected (by either writer or reader) than for most arguments. If we are not prejudiced to believe that administration is "all bad," at least we are predisposed to believe readily that it contradicts what is good in ministry. In any case, segregation is our favorite solution: keep those inferior debilitating elements where they belong and away from the purity of ministry.

In the last section of this chapter, I shall propose equality and integration. But I suspect that this argument will have much harder going. I shall claim that the elements of administration—in narthex conversation, in committee meeting, in telephone call, in writing agenda and memos—are vital encounters and valid occasions for creative ministry, even though they look a little different on the surface. I shall contend that these administrative encounters deserve full status membership among the occasions for ministry, on full equality with preaching, counseling, or picket lines. In fact, full integration is necessary, or the other forms of ministry are impoverished. Administrative encounters provide a uniquely vital occasion for the fashioning of ministry—be it pastoral, arousal to mission, or whatever—because they are occasions of immediate involvement in which minister and parishioner share a problem together.

Such will be my argument for equality and integration. But I expect as much resistance to such proposals among my minister readers as they are dismayed to find among their parishioners in opposition to proposals for social and racial integration. In each case, it seems to me, the resistance is primarily involuntary: administrative work somehow just doesn't "feel" as right or as good or as important. My proposals concerning administration may not turn out to be very sound, but it will be hard to reach that point in the argument to find out. Administration turns us off before we get to deliberate consideration.

When we do admit administration into the household of ministry, it is usually as a second-class servant, a kind of nanny or houseboy role, welcomed because necessary to sustain the high status roles, perhaps even beloved so long as its inferior status is kept clear. My suggestions later in this chapter, intending full integration and equal status, will be misunderstood by some as arguing for a servant-like supporting role for administration.

These then—if I have portrayed accurately in this section a common feeling about administration—are signs of prejudice. Can administration occasion dynamic give and take between persons, significant enlargement of ideas and purposes in peoples' lives, the gradual molding and fashioning of Christian ministry? No! (Can any good come out of Nazareth?) (Everyone knows what people from that section of town are like!) In these activities the minister feels trapped in the unworthy bustle on the edge of the Bethesda pool, and the only way to get where the healing action is— where pure ministry is—is to be picked up out of this hubbub and put into the pool. To try to say to him "pick up your pallet and walk," "where you are, in the midst of this busy confusion and without need to escape it into the pool, minister"—such a suggestion is alien and intolerable.

AN INTERLUDE: WRITING VS. ADMINISTRATION?

I have supposed that there may be some "prejudice" against the argument I want to advance at the end o this chapter: People will not gladly accept, or even consider, such an argument. What can I do about that? Is there some "administrative" way that I can move these allegedly "prejudiced" readers from their present position to the point where they will consider my coming argument?

If I don't undertake such administrative preparation, will the coming argument simply be lost? Do I have an administrative problem which needs to be dealt with to pave the way for the writing, but which also distracts from the writing? Should I stop writing and deal with this "administrative" problem. I might suggest a bibliography of reading, or refer such "prejudiced" objectors to a course of instruction, or to psychotherapy! I might write a memorandum to the publishers suggesting they not bother trying to sell the book to such people, or else suggesting particular kinds of advertisements which would attract them into the "congregation." I might modify my presentation so as better to win them to my audience. Whatever such administrative tactics, however, they would be resented as a distraction from the "ministry" on which I am intent.

But I would have dealt with the problem in such distracting "second-class" fashion because I would have already assessed it as a second-class problem. The substance of the writing—that's first-class—that's where the action is. The inconvenient details of dealing with people where they are, and bringing them to where the action is—that's supportive, second-class activity, necessary but incidental. "Sir, I have no one to put [them] into the pool . . ."

"Rise, take up your pallet, and walk." Maybe here, on the administrative fringes of action, there is substantial action, after all. Maybe encountering people in the annoying details of where they are is not so different, after all, from what minister or writer wants to do. Perhaps the "administrative problem" is integrated with the purposes and strategies of ministry. Perhaps ministry is not obstructed by such a problem but may be occasioned and advanced by it. The sections before and after this "interlude" attempt to discuss this "prejudice" directly, to deal with people where they are (or where I think some of them may be). In a sense such discussion is a distraction from my "pure" writing, directly advancing my argument. But I also think such discussion does advance the purpose of my writing, even though in a different form from what a "pure" writer would follow, for it attempts to feel the need to attend to the life situation in which readers and writers find themselves.

ONE SOURCE OF PREJUDICE: MISTRUST OF SELF

If a minister's reactions to administrative work are exaggerated and unrealistic in some ways such as that described above and labeled "prejudice"—or to the degree that they are, or when they are—this raises a question. What is it that "prejudices" a minister against administrative tasks so that he turns against them with exaggerated vengeance? The general thesis of this book suggests one interpretation that may apply to some ministers some of the time. It can be stated simply: Perhaps ministers devalue administration because that *is* what they do and do well.

Perhaps the best starting point for this discussion is to turn around the question that is most often asked about the dilemma. When researchers discover that ministers value least exactly what they spend most time at* (i.e., administration), the question most often asked is:

> Why do they spend so much time doing
> what they value least?

This kind of question is what leads to strategies for reducing the amount of time spent in administration—strategies which generally turn out futile. (Something in the minister, and/or his job seems to promote administrative work whatever tactics are taken to avoid it.) But suppose we ask the question the other way:

> Why does the minister value least
> what he spends most time at?

What if we supposed that the minister, in his *behavior*, perhaps intuitively, is responding to the valid call to ministry which is in administrative work (or more generally, is de-

---

* For example, Samuel W. Blizzard, "The Minister's Dilemma," *The Christian Century*, 73, 1956, pp. 508–9.

riving some important professional or personal satisfaction from it)? Then the question becomes something more like: Why, in his *evaluation*, does he turn against himself and what he is doing? Why does he repudiate what he spends two fifths of his time doing?

Is this a prime instance of the mistrust we feel about our circumstances (chapter 2) and our selves (chapter 3)? When we get restive with these administrative activities and keep saying we want to discard them so that we can get on with real ministry, how often are we mostly saying, "If I am doing it, it cannot be very important or effective." Or, "Whatever activities and circumstances I am now concerned with cannot be the best there is. There must be people and situations and encounters still awaiting me which are more likely occasions for ministry than anything I am involved with now."

Objectively viewed, these administrative tasks might be important and effective instances of ministry. But we are barred from making that objective assessment by the fact of our own involvement. Our own participation (and perhaps satisfaction) brings down the judgment of unworthiness. A common epithet for expressing this disparagement is: "administration."

The application of this epithet sometimes visibly escalates. Activities that seem to transcend "administration" and move into "ministry" themselves still get dubbed "administration." First it may be recruiting people and arranging for room and chairs for a discussion meeting on open housing that seems irksome. Then it may be having to sit with a human relations council steering committee to set agenda for a community-wide meeting. And even when one is engaged in the actual task of finding housing for people, or when one moves to positions of considerable power and influence —on the city council, or leading the church into building low-cost cooperative housing, or fashioning national denominational policies—there is still the temptation to feel that one is still on the verge, tending machinery, while the important action lies just beyond. The pool recedes as one advances. What we once fantasy as the next step which will put us into the swim, leaves us once we take it, still feeling on the verge. We often label this newly discounted activity administration.

Or first we may discredit the tedious "administrative" work of collecting book orders for a study group, or of arranging personal borrowing privileges at the nearby college library, while we long for "real" theological discussion or study. But then keeping the group or one's own study disciplined and on the topic seems to require routine "administrative" tactics of a sort that still seem to separate one from the heart of the study. But even immersed in the study, teasing out meaning seems to demand routines of collating, note-taking, cross-referencing, and analyzing which still seem mechanical, in a sense even "administrative" and still tantalizingly remote from the "real" work.

There is another clue that our mistrust of administrative work may sometimes imply a mistrust of self. It seems to make a difference whether the administration is mostly an individual responsibility or is part of a large institutional structure. Administrative work on one's own shoulders is what most often becomes the irksome albatross. But administrative work which is a well-defined and sanctioned part of an institution often seems a lighter yoke, much more bearable, precisely perhaps because it is in harness with something. The man who leaves a parish because its administrative burdens seem so unbearably distracting from ministry may turn to the "purer" ministry of college or hospital chaplaincy and engage cheerfully, even unnoticingly, in a far greater proportion of committee-attending, memo-writing, and telephonic-tending of machinery. The pastor who finds it most burdensome to keep the wheels turning in his church may find it an enjoyable relief to attend committee meetings of his council of churches or denominational structure or the board of visitors of his seminary or to engage in correspondence and other administrative activities related to these institutions. Our administrative drudgery often gains a validity and meaning from being part of a substantial institution which it doesn't enjoy so long as we are on our own.

Many of us are afflicted with a view of ourselves that makes it seem simply improbable that whatever we find ourselves doing can be significantly related to important goals. And we are afflicted with high standards and high aspirations which make it easy for us to measure our performance, whatever it is, as inadequate. It is much more consistent with our self-image to think of ourselves as still "on the verge," still in preparation and anticipation for the significant, "real" performance to come, still performing the administrative preliminaries and not the main event we want entered in the record book.

Perhaps what makes studying or preaching or counseling attractive and promising of significant accomplishment is that we are not doing it in large measure—yet! If we were or when we do spend more time and self in these activities, the same reservations creep in. We still can't fully invest ourselves, trust ourselves, expose ourselves in this particular encounter with city hall, this particular counselee, this particular reading or writing, this particular intensively prepared sermon series. These are still handled by temporary expedients and we still long—many of us, much of the time—for the right occasion still to come when we will be ready and able and the circumstances will be suitable. But so long as our ministry is functioning in large part in committees and conversations, in meetings and memoranda, it is these circumstances which we mistrust and devaluate and withhold ourselves from.

TAKE UP YOUR PALLET AND—*MINISTER!*

Caught in the disorderly hubbub of organizational chores, we need not gaze enviously at the nearby pool where there seems to be pure and vital ministry. The Lord comes and calls far more often where men are than where they look for him. When circumstances lead us into planning, organizing, troubleshooting, problem-solving kinds of activities and away from our preferred forms of ministry, perhaps they are to be respected, not disparaged, for doing so. Is ministry really to be found in neatly packaged roles, 30 minutes of preaching, 50 minutes of counseling, two hours of Bible study? These roles are abstractions, and they abstract minister and people out of life. Just because these are legitimate and useful abstractions and because minister and people function in them comfortably, they are not thereby normative for all of ministry. When the purposes of church and ministry, the knotty structural demands and trivial annoyances of institutions, the ambiguous purposes, limited visions, earnest but feeble faithfulness, and downright perversity of minister and people—when all these get tangled up together into minor and major crises, this may be the occasion that demands the most creative and virile of ministry. Here is where a real issue confronts real people. Perhaps it is not as grand an issue as those one would like to preach about, but it happens to be an issue where people—who are seldom as grand as one aspires to deal with—are. It is in the administrative snarls that one is far more likely to find passions aroused, masks lowered, neat roles abandoned, stubborn resistances revealed, and glimmering aspirations bared.

"Recruiting" people to a series of study or "dialogue" meetings is the time of encountering the mixture of aspirations, antagonisms, misunderstandings, yearnings, and apprehensions toward a more faithful life (which the study group may symbolize) which marks the present stage of their religious pilgrimage. Once safely captive in the study group, the spiritual growing edge may be dulled by the group's abstract and well-prepared routines.

The moment of spiritual crisis for a counselee is not so likely to be in the course of counseling, where matters follow reasonably predictable and manageable patterns, as it is in the agonies of "pre-counseling," when he is trying to decide whether he dares to offer his trust and confession to the minister and the God he speaks for. These are the critical, trivial, administrative, living encounters in which the minister does or does not reach into another's life with an element of grace.

It may be that purposes and direction for a congregation or a group get formulated decisively in the preliminary gropings for personnel and leadership and agenda and schedules. The minister who prepares carefully for his formal presentation at the opening session may long since have set the stage decisively and imparted more of his vision and impetus in the informal, hurried, "administrative" conversations by which he invited people to join the group.

A minister might develop forceful homiletical techniques and preach on God's grace for a lifetime without saying as much as he does in the way he greets an interruption during preparation of one of these sermons, or in the "trust" he shows a pre-teen-ager in leaving a message for his parents rather than calling back, or the "acceptance" he shows a harried man's reluctance to join the scout troop committee.

When a minister finds himself drawn into responding to the needs of a situation, perhaps he should be much readier than he usually is to respect the situation and his response to it as valid and significant in its own terms. To try to categorize an event as "administrative" or as "pastoral" *may* help to mobilize prepared attitudes and response patterns so as to deal effectively with the situation. But it may also, in arousing these prepackaged attitudes and responses, run the risk of missing altogether the occasion for ministry which the raw experience presents. The immediate response with which he intuitively tries to interpret and cope with events —even though it may seem routine and unexalted—may deserve to be trusted as ministry, without having to "elevate" the moment into the preconceptions and prepared responses of a "role." That pool may not have as much to offer as you already have going for you.

Call and purpose of ministry must first have arisen for

most of us in concrete situations. Our involvement and call may well have been obscured under such abstract considerations as deciding whether events are "pastoral" or "administrative." Responding again intuitively to an event in its own terms, without classifying it as "administrative" or not, may be a time of recapturing lost call and lost zest.

When a deacon is late for a deacons' meeting or has great difficulty in following the communion procedure, this may have an organizational meaning which might evoke the minister's special role as leader of an organization: the orderly activities are disrupted; the disruption may require some repair, for the sake of the general welfare and the purposes which the orderly activities serve. Such an event may also have a pastoral meaning: there may be some disruption in the man's personality or tension in his life which is interfering with his performance as a deacon and may invite pastoral attention and attempts at remedy. But there is a sense in which speculation about either such possibility is overlooking the more immediate and more obvious possibility. Right here and now, as *this* man participates in *this* communion service or *this* deacons' meeting, there may be something important happening in his life which accounts for this slight deflection in the smoothness of things and which is hinted at by the deflection. Disruptions, whether they be viewed as administrative problems or pastoral problems, occur for reasons, and these reasons may be much more immediate, much more pressing, much more urgent, much more meaningful, much more demanding of ministry than the organizational or personal difficulties they produce. Why can't a deacon serve at the Lord's table with equanimity? What anger, fear, guilt, unworthiness, or other attitude before the Lord may be betrayed by this difficulty at his table? A minister doesn't have to escalate his response to lay-training programs or liturgical reforms, or psychotherapy, or any other grand diagnosis and grand solution. The meaning of the event may be in the immediate confrontation. What is more, the purposes of ministry, which sometimes get expressed through administrative or through pastoral "roles," may be expressed more fully by abandoning or transcending these roles and attending to this immediate situation. What is required is not a new set of procedures or rules which are intended to get the deacon to the meeting on time or help him follow the service more smoothly. The minister doesn't have to retreat into such a formal "administrative" role. Nor is it required for the minister to start probing into the man's personal life and relations with his wife (even assuming that such personal upset may be distracting him). That would be retreat into a "pastoral" role. Each of these might seem better defined, and purer forms of ministry. But what if the minister can trust himself and the situation enough just to try to cope with it in its own terms, the kind of annoying troubleshooting, problem-solving activity he so easily resents as taking him from ministry (in its more abstract and purer forms)? What if he doesn't try to diagnose the difficulty into something he can minister to?

What if he just discusses the problem with the deacon: "It's hard for you to get the hang of this."

Addressed directly, not stiltedly and ministerially, and with the kind of trust expressed that his "problem" may be important in whatever terms he experiences it, the deacon may be ready to look at the situation himself: "This is different from anything I'm used to doing." From here, his sense of the difference and his awe of the difference can be naturally explored; perhaps his sense of how remote his life is from God will be set alongside the communion's assurance to the contrary. Whatever the direction taken, the result might seem to be some combination of administrative and pastoral activity, but will probably seem to minister and deacon to be neither. It will seem to each just more like a "good talk we had," and that will be ministry.

When a prospective Sunday school teacher excuses herself by telling of the turmoils in her life, this leaves an organizational problem of staffing the Sunday school, and one has to face the dilemma of turning on or turning off the administratively persuasive manner. It also invites pastoral attention to these professed turmoils. But the most immediate and simplest, and also the most significant question may be: Why is she telling me *these* things *now?* The instinctive, annoyed response (which he so carefully and ministerially suppresses) may not be far from the mark: Why drag all these personal matters into the simple question of teaching Sunday school? Why does she summon up *these* excuses in response to *this* invitation? What is the interaction between the prospect of teaching Sunday school and these difficulties in her life? Is teaching Sunday school so terrifying that she must resort to extreme excuses—and if so, why is it so terrifying? This is precisely a question for a minister and, in a sense, only for a minister—as distinguished from the administrative and pastoral questions which, in a sense, he borrows from the executive or the psychotherapist. Does she see Sunday school teaching as demanding that she pose as a model Christian which prompts her to set against this model the despair over her real life? Does Sunday school awaken memories of childhood experiences which she may somehow, secretly or otherwise, blame for her distresses? Could she be expressing, in this mild form, a kind of complaint: God doesn't deserve my service since he treats my life this way. The *immediate* and religiously most significant meaning the event has may be in terms of such interaction between this moment and the persistent themes of her own pilgrimage.

When the high school kids scar the newly painted walls, this raises the obvious organizational problems relating to the upkeep of the building, relations with other groups within the church, and the general welfare of the community of the church. It also raises possible pastoral or educational problems, relating to ebullience or rebelliousness or destructiveness or irresponsibility of the high school kids. But there also may be more immediate questions raised, combining these two perspectives, yet transcending both of them. Are the kids saying something about their attitude toward the formal structured household of faith which needs to be heard, or explicitly expressed, and responded to? Are the kids revealing something of their own irresponsibility in a way that is unmistakable and objective, demanding immediate attention? Need a minister shrink from the lessons which are in this episode for him and for the kids just because they come in the form of surprising, unplanned-for, annoying, petty, unmanageable, superficial, living problems? Why go off into the more abstract problems and solutions of wondering how to be a better "group leader" or a better educator or a better pastor or a better administrator? Why not respond in the most natural and intuitive manner to what *these* kids are doing and saying on *this* occasion?

To be a minister in such situations, one doesn't have to worry about outcome, or strategy, or techniques, or effectiveness, or the approval of superiors and constituents. One doesn't have to worry about evidencing the proper pastoral attitudes. There is a sense in which it is one's most immediate and open-eyed response, his most naïve curiosity that may come closest to the heart of the matter and be most faithful to the purposes of ministry. Anything else may be an evasion from the immediacy of the encounter into the more manageable structured roles.

"So what kind of a spot do those spots leave us in?" The minister may as well blurt it out the way he feels it.

"I guess Mrs. Moore will know we've been here. Can't hide us any more. Get it? No more, Moore."

"I think you mean 'no more Moore' . . . You feel underground?"

"Yeh, around here at least. You dig down to us once in a while. But that's about it."

"So you're going to climb out by climbing the walls?"

"No, man, those footprints are going to bury us. They're going to be dancing on our grave."

So the episode does "mean" something of significance in the lives of these teen-agers—if not so consciously in producing the footprints, more so in reflecting about them—

so long as they don't have to reflect through prescribed lenses. The "meaning" might be construed, later, in terms like alienation and search for belonging, testing the limits of God's (and minister's) patience, responsible membership in a community, guilt, apology, restitution, and many other terms. But such meaning never would have been reached, except by starting with the footprints, because in the footprints is where it was all registered.

A minister carefully and persistently guides his church into enlarged sense of mission. But he runs into snags. The missions committee asks the trustees to postpone repainting for one year and spend the money instead on an urgent and emergency ghetto project. When the trustees, angered, refuse ("We can't be irresponsible about our own property on a sudden whim."), the missions committee, equally angered, call for a church meeting to reform policies and procedures in controlling funds. ("Those trustees, who never even come to church, think it's their money instead of the church's.") The structure and the mission of the church are threatened, and the minister must spend much time in fence-building, reestablishing communication, listening to impassioned outpourings, arranging meetings, observing parliamentary procedures, revising bylaws. What a nuisance to be so grossly distracted from the ministry he was just getting well launched—the education of his people, through sermons, study groups, and service projects, into a fuller sense of mission. Now he must put all that off in favor of "administrative" troubleshooting and perhaps feel considerable bitterness about being let down by people who are supposed to act like Christians and don't.

Or is it possible that in this hectic politicking and patching he is, or can be, working much closer to the cutting edge between his people and their mission than he ever could in the ministry he now finds interrupted. "Well, just whose money is it? Let's talk about that!" Here is an issue that people are going to struggle with, fully involved, no holds barred. Perhaps they don't hear the overtones of stewardship in the minister's question which he would like to address and assume. If they take the question in terms of petty bickering, well, that is where they are and what is going to mobilize passions and searchings (as "stewardship" never could). If in searching to justify their answer to the question, they turn to criteria ("We put that money on the altar for God, not for the trustees." Or, "God may not have anyone to do his work if we don't keep his body here on earth healthy."), these still may not sound much like the seminary discussion of church as community of faith. But they are approximations which never would have been reached if the minister had started with the seminary-like discussion and tried to induce his people into it. And because in the politicking his ministry is where *their* passions are, these approximations carry a commitment, a clarity, and a permanence (perhaps even as a foundation for future development) which ministers undistracted by such disruptions may well envy.

Others who will envy will be those ministers beset not by passionate opposition but by indifference. When concern for mission is met by suburban inertia, here is another barrier to ministry which sometimes seems to invite administrative tinkering—organizing committees, study groups, projects in the church; joining a denominational committee on mission; finding a job in a more auspicious context. These more formal administrative responses are indeed distractions from—perhaps retreat from—the ministry of mission. *Perhaps* they will pave the way successfully for effective ministry—take minister and people from the verge and into the pool. But probably they won't.

But what about a more simple-minded, more direct kind of tinkering with the problem. If indifference and inertia greet the minister, perhaps this is what is to be directly confronted and examined. Indifference and inertia may be one kind of passion. There may be significant action and meaning, after all, embedded in the fact of indifference. This *is* a response people make, perhaps for reasons that are important for the minister to attend to, perhaps crucially central to the purposes of his ministry. What uncertainties of self, of faith, of others, what aspirations, what fears, what mixture of jumbled religious and personal gropings make it easiest for the person to confront claims to mission by turning them off. Why not find out by asking? Maybe not head-on provocatively, at first, until people are used to such ministry in naïve address to the thing-at-hand. The minister asks, casually, in a deacons' meeting, "I can get a rise out of the congregation if I preach on raising children, on the war, on sex, on politics, on practically anything. But when I talk about our responsibilities in the city, nothing. No fight, no interest at all. . . . Maybe I don't make myself clear."

"It *is* hard to know sometimes what you have in mind. These things aren't so close to us as our children, or the war even." Here is clear recognition of estrangement. This is no small confession and raises important questions needing, and apparently open to, exploration. It is apparently a relatively small step, not too difficult to take, from identifying indifference to acknowledging estrangement. Here in the indifference is where the estrangement is lodged and evidenced, and can be exposed. It would be a much longer step, one probably not often taken, from a sermon on estrangement to acknowledging estrangement.

"Just what is it you want us to do?" The indifference is converted into an obtuseness, inasmuch as the minister *has* made some concrete proposals. When the minister points *this* out, the obtuseness now invites further exploration, and in a few more steps, becomes identified as a certain degree of fear. "Well, I guess I'd rather not pay attention to those kinds of ideas." And the fear is now open to ministry.

The minister might labor mightily through the preaching role, first to bring people to church, then to develop text, phrases, illustrations, and delivery, then to organize a post-sermon discussion session—all to make his congregation feel the estrangement or fear he feels them to be caught in. Most ironically, a main objective in this program would be to overcome indifference. But chances are slight of getting past the indifference, into involvement with the text and message, and into intimate personal experience of estrangement or fear; and the minister's frustrations over indifference are likely to continue. "I have no one to put me into the pool" of genuine engagement with the lives of these people. Yet, perhaps the very indifference defines the engagement, to which the summons is warranted, "Take up your pallet . . ."

BECOMING
A MINISTER
AND
BECOMING
FREE

A minister lives in two worlds, but is more likely—if this book is rightly addressed—to feel comfortably at home in one more than the other. There is the transcendent world of values and norms, absolutes and ultimates, standards and criteria, visions of what ought to be and visions of what can be. Then there is also the immediate and immanent world of particular people and events, concrete relationships and specific involvements, decisions and outcomes, motivations and institutions. This manifest world reflects and expresses the transcendent. It must also be judged and fulfilled by the transcendent. The minister serves in a church and practices a ministry which he knows in terms of his vision of what is meant to be and should be. He also serves in a church which is another social institution and practices a ministry which is another social role, constricted by centuries of tradition and seemingly at odds with the transcending vision. He serves a church and practices a ministry defined by one set of people in one particular community, people he knows —especially himself—to be all too limited individuals.

The minister lives in both these worlds, but this book is speaking to the one who lives more comfortably in the former. He is such a loyal citizen of the transcendent world that he is far more aware of how the manifest disguises and perverts rather than expresses the transcendent. He is, accordingly, a reluctant citizen of the latter, the manifest here-and-now world in which he finds himself. Can any particular instance of preaching a particular sermon on a particular Sunday to a particular people—can arranging a particular agenda for a particular committee meeting on a particular evening—can any particular instance of ministry or of church in any way faithfully express the vision of church and ministry, which has called this particular occasion into being? The minister, at least the one to whom this book would speak, is predisposed to answer no and to withdraw or to withhold from these would-be expressions, judging them on behalf of the transcendent, rather dreamily hoping for another more faithful expression to come.

Such reservation is appropriate. The immediate world should never be confused with or lived in as assuredly as the transcendent. This would be idolatry, addiction, a destructive captivity, "hot bondage." It is undoubtedly the minister's faithful citizenship in the transcendent world and his discomfort in the manifest which has propelled him into the ministry in the first place and which makes him a good minister. He is so sensitive and loyal to the purpose and the value which calls life into being that he wants that life to come closer to realizing its purpose than he ever finds to be the case. This is what provokes and directs him into ministry. Persons with such a firm citizenship in the transcendent and discomfort in the manifest are right to find and to be found by this vocational role. This role presupposes just such persons, and they can be grateful that their early experiences of loyal citizenship to the first world prepares them for it.

But it also handicaps them in the exercise of that ministry. Their loyalty to the world of norms and standards prevents the free and joyous participation in the world in which that ministry must necessarily be. Such a minister is not able to live in the manifest world with the whole-hearted abandon with which he believes, for example, that God himself has entered the world; he is not able to make the transcendent come alive, nor even to recognize it when it has.

PORTRAIT OF THE MINISTER AS A YOUNG MAN

How does one come to live so earnestly and so desperately in the first world that he is uncomfortable in the second? To be sure, as already said, the ministry requires it. But also it seems plausible to suppose that the man comes to the ministry with this pattern, this citizenship already part of himself. Indeed, he may come to the role in part *because* this is already his pattern of life.

In other words, this book has presupposed that ministers —at least the ministers to which it is addressed—may share some more or less distinctive personality characteristics. It has presupposed that they share some more or less distinctive childhood experiences which have helped to prepare them to be the kind of persons and the kind of ministers that they are. As I have been writing, I have had a picture in mind of the kind of person I was writing to. Now it is time to expose and develop that picture, to make more explicit the presuppositions of personality characteristics and childhood background. I venture to present a composite psychological portrait and biography of the minister who is especially vulnerable to "cool bondage," especially vulnerable to copping out on the manifest world in steadfast loyalty to the transcendent, especially unable to let himself go.

It is, if you will, a riskily specific portrait which will match, in all details, no one. But it may still seem familiar. I believe that most readers who have found the earlier part of the book speaking to them or about them—hence, most readers who have come this far—will be able to recognize themselves in this portrait and biography. If they do, perhaps this will help them, as it helps me, to understand their proneness to ministry on the verge (including the inevitable feeling of being on the spot), by seeing this proneness in the larger context of a personal orientation established by earlier experiences. Perhaps it will help them, as it helps me, to understand and accept these characteristics by seeing them shared with many of their fellows. Perhaps such perspective can help to shift the emphasis from "ministry on the *verge*" to "*ministry* on the verge." I don't expect anyone to be released from the haunting awareness that his ministry is only on the verge or that he can ever escape fully from being on the spot. But even there, on the verge, where one is more or less fated to remain, he can still find unapologetic ministry.

As always, investment into one particular, in this case investment of pages of this book into the description of a particular pattern of personal development, risks much incompleteness and irrelevance. It would be safer, but also less useful, to be more general and inclusive. If the reader feels that what follows has no relation with his own experience, or if he feels that childhood experiences have no relevance to understanding what goes on in adult professional life, then I hope he will be willing to overlook the remainder of this book. Perhaps the earlier chapters can still stand on whatever validity they may have in themselves. If the reader can forgive the extra 25 cents or so the following pages may have cost him, I will not regret the time, effort, and risk I have ventured in trying to flesh out the earlier chapters with this one.

THE LITTLE ADULT

By what earlier experiences, through what processes, might a person become such a faithful representative and spokesman for the world of "shoulds" and "oughts" that he is a reluctant participant in the world of "is"? One place

131

to look for the minister who is the earnest custodian and spokesman for the "ought" and the "meant to be" may be in the school boy who finds the values and the standards he has learned from adults (and presumably the approval from adults which has backed them up) very important in his life, perhaps more important and more congenial even than the values and the friendship of his schoolmates. Such a school boy already is living in two worlds. One is defined by these expectations he has (largely acquired from parents) as to how life ought to be. The other is defined by the actual daily experience (largely in relation with agemates and sometimes encountered with dramatic suddenness at the onset of school) as to how life is.*

When a minister comes from seminary, or from summer retreat, to face the people and programs of his church, and when these confrontations trigger in him apprehensions over the huge gulf between these people and programs and the values to which he has become committed during his training and retreat—perhaps this minister has already been through this experience many times before. For example, these may be the same apprehensions he felt when he left home and entered kindergarten, when he left home and began attending teen-age parties, when he left home for college—every time with the same reservation as to how much his involvement in the new world here will contradict the values and the relationships to which he is firmly committed.

Rules (and the goodwill of rule-makers) are important. Being disciplined by adults or being expelled from a group for rowdiness would bring devastating chagrin. If he can play it cool enough to preserve the goodwill of schoolmates, so much the better. But where contradiction is unavoidable,

---

* Empirical evidence as to the commonness of such characteristics among clergymen is presented in my "Psychological Characteristics of Religious Professionals," a chapter in *Research on Religious Development: A Comprehensive Handbook*, ed. Merton P. Strommen (New York: Hawthorn, 1970).

the peers must give way to the adults and their values. Here is the boy assigned by the teacher to be monitor in her absence, the crossing guard at the street corner, the usher in the noon-time movies, always the *responsible* boy. He is not in the group that act up while the teacher is out or who huddle and chatter while waiting to be allowed across the street. He is generally excluded—because he has excluded himself—from the little delinquencies and truancies the other boys cook up. This is not necessarily with ill will on either side; it is just recognized that this is not something he gets involved in. His role in life is different. He is the one that adults may cite as the model they want other boys to follow. Substitute teachers and baby-sitters are people to be appeased, not to be plotted against.

Friends tend to be those which correspond with parents' wishes; so do after-school activities, hobbies, the hours he keeps, habits, courses in school and the grades earned in them. A boy is not necessarily consciously aware of making these choices so as to win parental approval. He is already too thoroughly initiated into his parental world of values to need to do that. It just happens that, in reflecting backward on these choices, they all seem to have come out to correspond with parental preferences.

He is more accustomed to living in the adult world than getting involved in the peer world. Sitting around while adults talk is not an uncommon way to spend an evening. His opinion is trusted and consulted when family decisions are to be made. In school activities, his role tends to be like that of an adult leader or an adult observer. He might be editor of the school paper or a debater, be manager of a team, be treasurer or historian of a group, judge in an honor court. He is appointed by adults and even elected by his peers to such positions as student government because his role as mediator (minister?) between adult world and peer, between adult values and peer, is recognized by both sides. He can get along with adults better than most students and he can represent the adult values to the students. (If student office is purely a popularity contest, then, of course, some-one else is elected.) He is much more likely to be in officially sponsored and adult-supervised activities than in more spontaneous peer-organized groups. He probably feels out of the social whirl which largely dominates life for many of his childhood and adolescent classmates.

This may have something to do with why he gets actively involved in church youth groups. Like the school, the church provides occasion for exercise and recognition of leadership roles in which he becomes especially adept and on which he is particularly reliant. But the church also may provide something that he misses in school. Here is a peer group moving at a less fast pace, better integrated with the world of adult values. Here is a clearly adult-sponsored and adult-sanctioned peer group—something of an anomaly and a rarity in the adolescent world—oriented toward the all-important adult values, but also more or less guaranteeing esteem from peers. It is an exaggeration to say that the church youth group becomes a haven for the socially inept or immature. But it may be particularly attractive and prominent in the life of those who need encouragement and guidance in developing peer relationships without having to sacrifice adult goodwill or membership in the adult world, a sacrifice that peer involvements outside the church group generally demands.

In short, we are describing the *little adult*, the child who is alerted to, loyally committed to, proficient in advocating and practicing the values of the adult world. His frame of reference, as he moves through the world of childhood and adolescence, is the adult world which transcends childhood and adolescence.

The ministry, then, may become the natural extension of this role in life. For such an adolescent, projecting his vocation, the pulpit seems an appropriate place to be. He can continue to be a spokesman and custodian among his peers for the transcendent values. It seems as though one can continue this familiar and presumably satisfying role without having to sacrifice the goodwill of other persons. He anticipates that he will be able to function largely independently as a kind of adult-like leader of others, but still as a member of a sanctioned social institution that tends to supply the kind of warrant and support that adults have always served in his life.

The minister would seem to have a kind of guaranteed access into the lives and homes of people, perhaps an important advantage for one uncertain about his social skills with peers. But this is true with two qualifications important to the adolescent we are portraying. For one thing, the persons in the church with whom he foresees himself relating tend to look more like the adults with whom he is more comfortable than his peers. Secondly, ministers' relationship with people is more or less formally defined, not unduly demanding of the personal social skills the adolescent may feel shaky about. If he is unsure how to enter social groups, he can enter as minister; the role is provided.

Such, we conjecture, may be some of the appeals the ministerial role may have for the boy coming up through the childhood and adolescence we have described. But if so, these same characteristics help us to understand why it is difficult for him to make the leap of investment, to trust himself getting thoroughly involved in any circumstances or relationships. There remains a primary allegiance to and greater experience in, the more formal structure and the highest expectations.

LEARNING TO LIVE ON THE VERGE

So perhaps we have described something the reader may recognize to be part of his own experience and perhaps we have described something which can be recognized as a kind of childhood and adolescent anticipation of the feeling of the minister of being on the verge. Even if the preceding is an accurate and useful portrayal for some persons, it still leaves one important question. The picture so far doesn't go very far toward explaining how the boy comes to develop these patterns in the first place. How and why does he come to be early in life a loyal citizen of the adult world of values in a way which predisposes him to become a loyal citizen of the larger universe of values? The answer to this question is far more conjecture than the material in this chapter so far. But it may be worth venturing because it may help to understand more of the basis for this pattern, especially the *earnestness* of the commitment to the world of "oughts" and the corresponding *timidity* about entering the world of "is." Or it may help to do this for some readers. Others, as before, are invited to abandon this particular limb onto which the book trails off.

The answer might be the fairly obvious one: perhaps this is a boy for whom adult relationships and adult approval have become very important, but for whom these important satisfactions have remained precarious and never assured. If so, we could understand why he persists so strongly in his allegiance to adult values as a token of adult approval.

The minister I am describing is likely to have come from a family in which he had a close but never highly satisfying relationship with his parents. He is more likely than not to be the first or only child in the family, meaning that he becomes accustomed to the parents' undivided attention and more importantly, they are eager to give it and to foster his dependence on them. New parents do much hovering and caretaking and also, later on, exert pressure to do well and to be good. New parents are also likely to be inexperienced and reticent about expressing freely and openly the signs of affection they may have induced a particularly strong need for. Chances are good that the boy has skipped a grade or moved from town to town frequently (perhaps as the son of a clergyman or other transient) in his early school years, leaving him relatively more reliant on parent and family than on peer relationships. If his father is away from home much (for example, as salesman, clergyman, or physician) or is otherwise aloof and relatively inaccessible, this puts more uncertainty into parental support and also drives a boy into relatively stronger relationships with his mother. From her he is more likely to acquire the kind of values he will find most endorsed by teachers, and most in conflict with his schoolmates, and also the nurturant values which will serve him well in a pastoral role. From his father he might have acquired attitudes and guidance—a role model if you wish—that would have led him more easily into involvement in the boys' world.

Another way of understanding this conjectured dilemma of having needs for parental (and perhaps particularly, maternal) attention and affection strongly aroused but never surely satisfied may have to do with understanding what a child means to the mother. Along with a boy particularly reliant on his parents may be a parent particularly reliant on the child. Especially if he is the first child, especially if the family moved much and if the father is frequently away or aloof, especially if the child was long awaited or otherwise especially welcomed, the mother will be particularly attentive, solicitous of every whimper, giving surveillance to every action, holding high aspirations for every stage of the boy's development. But such attention arouses a dependent relationship higher than any parent can persistently and unconditionally sustain. She is bound, perhaps for the same reasons that made her turn especially to the boy, not to be regularly able to deliver the kind of support she has trained the boy to expect and even need. Furthermore, her own expectations and aspirations may be so high, that the boy is bound to fail her with a disappointment which shows as her withdrawal and decreased support for the boy. Perhaps even any effort he makes is doomed to failure by her high aspirations. "Can't you give Mommy a kiss more like you really mean it?" "The notes are right on the piano, but now watch the fingering." "I'm glad you're so busy at school, but I do miss you around home." Or, "Don't you think you should get out of the house more and into more things?"

In other words, specific ventures of involvement in one

activity or another fail to yield, for the boy, anything like support. The "transcendent" values and meanings (which at this early stage of life tend to be identified with parental support) which he wants to find *in*, or by means of, particular involvements and expressions of life are not available in them. He cannot trust these particular involvements as a means of relating himself to what for him at the time is a basic source of his life. The two worlds do not, in fact, merge for him. His ventures into the spheres of particular involvements and activities, his investments of himself, threaten rather than confirm his membership in the first world. As he may feel it, he wants to please his mother and feel close to her wishes and warmth by doing things. But doing things doesn't pay off after all. The accomplishment doesn't bring the sense of assurance, because she hasn't been able to deliver the assurance unconditionally. So the only way to be sure of being near her wishes and warmth is the more direct solution of being near her.

Once the boy has learned that he has to stay close to home base—even at the expense of being called a "goal-sticker"—in order to guarantee the sense of backing and support he needs, it is difficult for his attitudes to be changed by even the most earnest conviction of the doctrine of incarnation or of God's immanent working in history, by theories of existentialism, or by secular theologies. He will do his best to "get involved" in the particularities in which he finds himself. He may spend himself effectively and energetically, but risk and freedom are not the fruit of willing, and the man we have been describing will still be afflicted with a yearning for the more immediate direction and assurance beyond the verge. It is the very human dilemma of being on the spot. And it is the place of ministry.